The Myth of the Yellow Kitchen

The Myth of the Yellow Kitchen

A Memoir

RHOADA WALD

Dear Katy: [illegible]

Merrmack Media
Cambridge, Massachusetts

Library of Congress Control Number: 2014946872

ISBN: print: 978-1-939166-51-7

ISBN: ebook: 978-1-939166-52-4

This book was printed in the United States of America

Published by Merrimack Media, Cambridge, Massachusetts
Summer, 2014

Many thanks to my children and their spouses—
Marian and George, Anne and Steve, Beth and John

And to my grandchildren—
Todd, Megan, Justin, Jonathan, Michael, and Jake

Contents

Prologue   xi

Part I. The Legacy of Divorce

1. The Myth of the Yellow Kitchen   3

2. Midnight Awakening   9

3. Calling the Calendar in Supreme Court   13

4. Head of The Household   17

5. The Legacy of Divorce   21

Part II. Family Matters

6. I Love Mothering   27

7. Thanksgiving Feast   35

8. The Sweater   37

9. Generations   45

10. Who Talked to Him Last?   47

11. Mourning   55

12.	Memories and Memorabilia	*63*
13.	The Waiting Room	*69*

Part III. Milestones

14.	The House	*81*
15.	The Empty Nest: A Second Time Around	*93*
16.	About Men: The Recurrent Dilemma	*97*
17.	Mirror, Mirror on the Wall	*105*
18.	I Want	*109*

Part IV. Challenge and Choice

19.	Finding My Own Road–The Working Life	*113*
20.	The Dawning of Liberation	*119*
21.	In Jerusalem	*123*
22.	Assignment in India	*129*
23.	Unfinished Business	*143*
24.	Disappointing Moves	*151*
25.	The Passover Seder: A Search for Freedom	*153*

Part V. Resolution

26.	Things Matter	*163*
27.	Worry	*169*
28.	Reflections on Worry	*173*

29.   Tenants In Common—An Adventure In Living   175

30.   Adventure and Challenge   181

31.   On the Sebug River in Connecticut   185

32.   Epilogue   187

      Acknowledgements   193
      Favorite Memories By My Family   195
      Author Profile   205

Prologue

This book began in 1964 as an aftermath of my divorce. The actual writing began sixteen years later when I sold my house and stood in that kitchen for the last time. I had come to broom-sweep the house, to get it ready for the closing that would take place the following day.

I stood in the kitchen, walked through the empty rooms, and thought about the last twenty-eight years in our house, what happened there, who we were, my children and I, and who we became. As I went from room to room, recalling our family and the people who passed through and gave meaning to our lives, I talked into a tape recorder. I needed to take away some concrete symbol of our lives there, something of the past to hold onto in the future.

The house I was selling had been our refuge and shelter during and after the divorce. Now it was time to sell, the market was good, and my children were grown and living on their own. I changed my mind several times. The only relief I found from the inner turmoil about selling or not selling came from writing. The tapes I made the day before the closing in the empty house became my first poetry. In one form or another I have been writing ever since—poetry, professional writing, letters, short essays. This book is a compilation of those essays written over a long time and collected here thematically rather than in chronological order.

I grew up believing "till death do us part." I had no long-range career goals, I only wanted to be a wife and mother. That was my dream.

But life is not so simple. And my dream came true, but only for a short time. This book is about my journey and my understanding of the hardships and the triumphs. It is about a young woman from New York, first generation American, who started out quite traditionally, like so many women of my generation, and was forced to take an unconventional road. I changed in some unexpected ways, in my goals, aspirations, beliefs, and mostly, in my internal view of myself and the world. This is my voice, sometimes troubled, often exhilarated, always struggling and thinking about meaning and the next step.

The divorce changed my life and who I am.

I was twenty when we married and thirty-seven when we divorced. Within the span of seventeen years, I had a number of jobs, earned a master's degree in education, and then taught for several years. The highlights of those years though, were our children. We had three, Marian, Stephen, and Beth. But after the divorce, I had to figure out a career route that was satisfying and remunerative. I also had to learn how to navigate the "adult single world."

Eventually I acquired a doctorate and was involved in new settings of higher education which led to several opportunities to live and work abroad, consulting in India, Cyprus, and Israel. Some of the writing in this book evolved from the letters I wrote home as I tried to capture the meaning of being alone and fending for myself, the images of the people and places, the spirit of the adventure, and my fears.

Although this is my story, it also reflects a broader cultural phenomenon. This was the beginning of the feminist movement, a time when the family structure was in great flux, which impacted male and female roles. It was a time when more women were working outside the home and divorce was no longer a rarity. I was the first person in my circle of friends to get a divorce, but over the next few years, many people I knew were going through the same experience.

I hope that in reading this book you, the reader, will find some comfort in the possibility that crisis can lead to growth, new pathways, and fulfillment.

PART 1

The Legacy of Divorce

I believed that yellow is the color of happiness
cheerfulness, the color of life and sunshine.

1

The Myth of the Yellow Kitchen

I believed in the myth of the yellow kitchen for a very long time. Actually, I believed in it until I was thirty-seven years old. As long as I can remember, back to the early grades, I would sit and scribble the same thing over and over. It was a simple house, with a front door and two windows on one side and two on the other. I always painted or drew the house in the same way, and if the kitchen wasn't yellow, the curtains on the windows were.

I believed that yellow is the color of happiness, cheerfulness, the color of life and sunshine. A yellow kitchen always symbolized the beauty of family and marriage "till death do us part." My parents also believed in the myth, in fact, I learned it from them. Their marriage was terrible, but they still managed to convince us that the myth was real.

My story starts in the Bronx, one of the five boroughs in New York City. Both my parents came to the United State as toddlers. They were first generation, American Jewish parents who were not educated but did well and were middle class. They came from the immigrant dream to discard Old World habits and become American.

Unfortunately, they were not suited to one another and the dream of living happily ever after certainly didn't take place in our home. The household alternated between their periods of disagreements that sometimes turned violent followed by tension and shorter periods of rapprochement and peace.

My parents' aspirations for their children were their aspirations for themselves. I was the eldest of four, followed by a sister and two brothers. My father was a businessman, and we were well-fed, housed in a variety of wonderful houses, and dressed in the latest styles. American and Jewish rituals permeated our family life. My mother was an excellent hostess and cook, and our homes represented the quintessential middle class of those times. They had made it in America.

The first house I remember was a four-family home owned by my grandparents. We lived on the second floor, and my grandparents lived on the third. When I came home from school, if my mother wasn't home, I would go upstairs to my grandmother, who would welcome me with kisses, milk, and a cookie. The school was on our corner and when we had a fire drill, my grandfather would walk in front of us and wink at me. I would shyly glance back.

I can still picture the steps of that house, the old red bricks, and the hard-to open windows. Perhaps this house was a tenement—it doesn't exist anymore but whatever it looked like, I remember that this house was the home of kisses and cookies, of love, safety, and security.

Eventually, we moved west to another part of the city, decidedly a step up economically and class-wise. My father was beginning to make money in the sausage casing business, and traveled often. His car was the longest and shiniest on the block. Our new home was in a large two-family house my parents purchased. We lived on the first floor, a palace with four bedrooms, a dining room, and a living room.

I had my own room, my own special room that I could decorate any way I wanted. I picked out yellow, floral wallpaper. I remember my disappointment when the wallpapering was finished. It didn't turn out the way I expected. It wasn't what I had dreamed, but then what is. My romantic dream of living in a yellow flowered room just never came to pass. Where do those dreams and fantasies of beauty come from?

I always have a desire to go back to important places and several years ago I went back to see that house. Now, it was a ten family tenement, once so proud, now dilapidated and not cared for. Dreams do have a tendency to turn to nightmares in real estate as well as relationships.

My brother, five years younger than I, was a sickly infant, he had many allergies, and the doctor urged my parents to get him out of the city during the summers. That began our long odyssey and wonderful summers in Lake Mohegan, near Peekskill, New York. Until we went there for the first time, I had known only rectangular blocks or streets, the stone stoops we sat and played on, the red lights, and the tiny grocery store on the corner. Suddenly we were in a new world with trees and grass. Our neighbors were not upstairs but in the next house, one on the left and one on the right.

Our first house at the lake had an icebox, and ice was delivered several times a week. There was also a kerosene stove. It had a wonderful screened porch, and even now I remember the early morning noises when I slept out there during a hot summer night. That porch had old armchairs that were great for curling up with a good book. I still yearn for another house with a screened porch and, paradoxically, have never lived in one since then.

Despite my parents' tumultuous relationship, we had glorious times during those summers. My parents tried to grow things, corn, tomatoes, even cantaloupe once. As children, we were free to explore the community, ride our bikes, go on hikes, start a club, and write a newspaper. There were no camps or supervision, so different from the lives of my grandchildren where almost every moment seems organized. A free spirit was in the air.

As I grew up, there were generally accepted expectations. Although my parents had not completed high school, we would go to college. My brothers would have careers. My sister and I would find Jewish husbands. I never remember anyone asking me where I wanted to go and how I was to get there. I never asked myself. I just drifted along from high school to college hoping it would all be decided somehow by graduation. And it was, one month after I graduated from college, I was married. I just turned twenty.

The man I married, Charly, was an ex-G.I entering college whom I met at a dance in Lake Mohegan. He lived in Peekskill, a town a few miles from the lake. I was intoxicated with his quietness, his apparent gentleness, a welcome relief after the bombastic home I came from. He was very different from my father. We married just six months after we met. We thought we knew each other, but in six months it is really difficult to know anyone.

I worked for several years at insignificant jobs which, combined with the G.I. bill, financed Charly's undergraduate education. While he completed graduate school, I earned a master's degree in education to help him through the last years.

After I married, my first kitchen was indeed yellow, a bright, canary yellow, the color of eternal romance that I'd been dreaming about. We were married and cheerfully doing all the things that people do starting out. He was building a career, and I was helping him, first working while he studied, and later working part-time while I took care of the children.

I believed that suburbia and all the dreams of the yellow kitchen came true.

Charly and I both loved babies. First, there was Marian, the daughter I always wanted. Then Stephen, a year and a half later, and Beth five years after Stephen. Together, we would both get up in the middle of the night, no matter whose turn it was, to give the night feeding.

It seemed that there could be a home with peace and love and kindness to children, along with friends, fun, masquerade parties, dinner parties, vacations, and the good life.

The yellow kitchen magnified was now a part of a larger dream. We were doing all the things we had dreamed about together, having children, living in suburbia, building careers, developing wonderful friendships, and watching our children grow.

Perhaps, in reality, it all changed very gradually, but as I look back now, it seems as if suddenly, my world changed color. Yellow fades so quickly, and gentleness can explode with an unexpected rage. The marriage was over. Where had I been in my dream? Was I color-blind? How come I didn't see that the colors were changing? What was once a dream changed into a nightmare, and bright yellow changed to brown, almost gray really.

What happened to that gentle, quiet husband? Was the myth of the yellow kitchen a dream that couldn't live up to its promise? Do all dreams fail? Or, was it my fault? Did I fail? How?

2

Midnight Awakening

Today is July 15th 2013; I am sitting on my patio looking at cars passing by, staring at the beauty of the building across the street, scanning the people walking below. In this peacefulness, my mind wanders back to a long night in 1964 the third night alone with my three children, Marian was nine, Stephen eight, and Beth three.

That night in 1964 was another night of sleeplessness, the sleeplessness that began with Charly's demand for a divorce. For three months the house felt like a war zone, with tension, no privacy, and the continuous harangue and assault, "I want a divorce. I want a divorce, now."

At that time in New York State there was some barbaric legal custom that did not permit husband or wife to leave the marital home until the divorce agreement was settled or some agreement regarding marital obligations was clear. Negotiations about divorce, financial distribution, and custody of the children are not issues that can be resolved overnight. During that time, Charly slept in a different room, was gruff with the children, and would not eat with us. The children were nervous, not really understanding the meaning of the change. Frankly, I could not comprehend what was happening either. What happened to that gentle, tender man I married?

The tension during that time was unbearable, and sleeplessness was always a symptom of my distress. This was another night of lying awake, turning, tossing, trying to sleep. But now he was finally gone.

It was the middle of March. I was in bed listening to the trees swaying, brushing against the house, the rain pounding on the roof. From my window, I could see branches strewn over the lawn, in the middle of the street, and in front of our house. A few of the streetlights were out and the ones remaining cast a dull light on the sidewalks. Except for those few streetlights, I didn't see a light anywhere. And even if I did, whom would I call and for what? It was two o'clock in the morning. Now alone in the house with three children, I was frightened as I had never been before.

Just a few days ago, I could hardly wait for him to leave and have some peace. But, I still wasn't accustomed to the emptiness of the big bed, slightly tilted without his weight. I listened to the wind whirling outside, and was the furnace vibrating louder than usual? I listened for the children. I had a pain in my stomach, a headache over one eye, I could hardly breathe. I went over and over the same questions. How had this happened? Will I survive? How?

In the midst of my mind's wanderings, I heard Beth cry out. I ran to her to discover that she was sick, really sick. She was only three; her temperature had risen to 104 degrees.

I phoned the doctor. I only reached his service, but thankfully he immediately called me back. Beth was losing consciousness, I told him. He said "fill the tub with warm water, put Beth in it and wait until her temperature goes down."

The bathtub was downstairs, I ran down, leaving Beth lying listless in her bed. I filled the tub with warm water, running up and down, alone in the night to check on her. Finally, I carried her down, hot, feverish, and softly whimpering. We were both weeping, she in the warm tub, me kneeling on the cold tile beside her, soothing her, gently bathing her with the warm water, brushing away my tears. In what seemed an eternity, she was cooler. At last, I carried her upstairs, put her night clothes on, and soothed her until she fell asleep.

But I didn't sleep. I lay there until early morning, listening to the wind in the trees, hearing the early morning noises, tears still flowing. I couldn't stop them, remembering how frightened I had been earlier that night, thinking about my life, the divorce, what happened. Still shaking, my body was in turn hot and cold, I had to change my clothes. I checked on Beth and Steve and Marian as well. In this night of terrible nights, anything could happen. Beth was better, she felt cool to the touch, and Marian and Steve were sleeping quietly. I survived the night. Beth and I survived together and, now, in the early morning, things seemed calmer, anything was possible.

That night alone with the three children, I realized a phase of my life was over. I had to take responsibility. I had to take care of the divorce, protect myself and my children, pay the bills, fix what was wrong in our dilapidated but wonderful 1920's house, make decisions, run a household, be two parents. There was no one to help. In one night that began with paralyzing fear, I began to understand that I had to earn a living, raise three children, take care of the squirrels in the roof, maintain the lawn, and call the plumber. And what I didn't know, I would learn.

Finally, the wind died down, Beth was safe and I began my journey into adulthood. A nightmare became a rebirth.

3

Calling the Calendar in Supreme Court

Bond vs. Bond
Cohen vs. Cohen
Plaintiff present
Defendant present.

Dannerfield vs. Dannerfield
McKenna vs. McKenna
Conference, Your Honor
Conference, Your Honor.

Bagdalino vs. Bagdalino
Wald vs. Wald
Present, Your Honor
Second Call, Your Honor.

Etcetera vs. Etcetera
Rhythms reminiscent of
melting pots
and marriage vows
Now, adversaries
for alimony
child support

and custody
of the children.

Long hours waiting
Crowded corridors
hard seats
plastic coffee cups.
Waiting for the calendar.
Number 11
Number 14
Today, tomorrow,
this afternoon.

Smart suits
standing, talking
knowing each other,
laughing.
Clients sitting,
sagging in the long wait,
waiting for the life battle
for alimony,
child support,
and custody of
the children.

A woman paces
long blond hair
slit skirt,
high-heeled shoes.
Party clothes and
angry eyes.

"The system,
the fucking system.
Those bastards,
all of them.

Contracts with no meaning
Never paying,
fighting, fighting
for everything.

Waiting and fighting.
What a system!"

A man talks
of an ordinary day.
coming home
finding
their furniture gone,
his wife gone,
the children gone,
and the gas jets on.

"My children
like hostages,
brainwashed.
Seven months
I haven't seen
my children."
Today, they meet
in Courtroom A.
"Will they want me?
Will they like me?
How are my children?"

My turn with
a former spouse.
Five people in
a courtroom.
The black robe
and smart suits
leave.
We are alone,
married in our youth,
now silent.

He sits
I sit
He from another life,
a life
having nothing to do
with alimony,

child support,
or custody of the children.

Winners and losers
losers and winners
losers everyone
The rawness,
intensity and power
of former lovers
in their life battles
for alimony
child support
and custody of
the children.

4

Head of The Household

After the divorce, my place in the family, rank, order, and serial number, was head of the household. Actually, it was the Internal Revenue Service who gave me that label and defined my status as a person with some entitlement. According to the IRS, the Head of the Household is someone who is neither married nor single, but has responsibility for others, literally, the head of the household. The entitlement, of course, relates to allowances toward taxes for being responsible for all those people, but for me, it was an identity. Maybe it wasn't much, but it was something.

The negotiations for the divorce were appalling. I may have needed advocates before in my life, but this was my first experience with the male legal world—the lawyers, judges, ex-husband, even a male psychiatrist. I was pressured by all of them including the psychiatrist, to settle. Actually, I became head of the household as soon as my husband left the house, but legally, I didn't bear that title until the divorce became final.

That first summer I took the children to summer camp; I had a job as camp mother with free tuition for the children. That was the turning point. I was in a new setting with new people who did not know I was a failure, who perceived me as an adult, an adult with responsibilities. My transformation had begun.

My home now consisted of my three children, various women of varying ages, who stayed for varying amounts of time taking care of the children and the household while I went to work.

That first year I began to learn what being head of the household really meant. Along with the tax entitlement, there were certain other benefits that accrued from this lofty status. As head of the household I was entitled to make all the decisions about what to eat, when to go to bed, should the lawn be cut, and if so, by whom. Once I was invited to Fire Island with the children by a male bachelor friend. He couldn't get over all the decisions I made in an hour. "Could I go into the water now? Could I have a cookie? When are we going home?" In a very short time, though, it was a breeze—not the single life, but making decisions.

The IRS gave me a title, but they didn't help very much with the worry about money. If anything, they made it worse. As head of the household, I was also the fountainhead of worry. Who else was entitled to such pleasures? The worries descended on my shoulders, head, mind, soul, and body. Sometimes my body was so tired from worry I couldn't even relax to sleep.

The main thing I worried about was money. I had all the financial obligations now, even health care, for my children. There was never enough money. I was divorced before the divorce laws in New York State provided an equal share of the combined assets to the wife. My divorce settlement was anything but just in relation to what I had contributed over the years and my children's needs. Each month I engaged in the great juggling game, which bills to pay, which to include in the "next month" pile. Several times I borrowed from a relative; once it was $2,500, and it took me years to pay it back.

At first I was two people, one the person who acted as if I were the head of household, but inside felt frightened, almost panicky. The other woman was growing proud, forceful, learning to have confidence in herself, leaving the panic behind, what I didn't know I would learn.

Time of course helped. Time gave me courage to find the optimism and experience. At the darkest moments, I would be reassured by telling myself that "this problem will be better next year. By this time next year, all these problems will be resolved."

There was also help. Several women along the way who knew and loved me, women who believed in me, encouraged me always. "Yes you can, you can do it. You can raise the children, get the doctorate, and forge a career."

Long ago, I believed that therapy was a sign of inadequacy, failure, or inability to cope. But now I know that the individuals with courage to face the real issues in their lives go into therapy. I believe it was my strength and resiliency, my desire to survive, my desire to do more than survive that led me to therapy.

I wouldn't want anyone to think that being head of the household is all bad. It has its good points, fun moments even. First, you're free to do whatever you want, go out, cook or not cook, experiment with living, with men, with sex. You are so liberated you are even free to make mistakes or fail at something. After all, I was the head of the household, I could even fail. Heads of household also decide how children should be brought up, disciplined strictly, or with love, kindness and some degree of rationality.

All in all, being head of the household was terrifying at first, but I got used to it. To tell the truth, I really liked it. Now, I could never be second in command.

5

The Legacy of Divorce

The legacy of divorce
means peace at home.
Nobody to quarrel with,
No one to tell you you're not
bringing the children up right.

Why did you give them a cookie?
Why could they watch television?
How come they have ice cream
at this hour of the night?

You're free to do whatever you want.
Fix something here
Build bookshelves there.
Paint the walls whatever color.

You can experiment with sex
With love, with men.
You can find yourself
without permission.

You can travel
wherever you want,

Have friends in
Cook, or not cook.

But the children
The children want a father
Need a father
Where's the father?

When something wonderful happens
a birthday or a graduation
or a child is in a play.
You want someone to share it with
to go with, to exult with.

Yesterday, now, tomorrow,
Grandchildren, weddings.
When to meet, how to meet
Not to meet
Everyone tense
The legacy of Divorce

Worlds Apart

1947

Working in Israel — 1987

PART 2

Family Matters

With my grandchildren — 1997

Our home was about growth, people growing up,
me growing up, all of us young, finding our way,
searching, exploring, and questioning.

6

I Love Mothering

I love mothering. I loved watching the children grow and seeing how different they were from each other, their interests, their passions.

Charly and I both loved babies and we would watch them in their cribs, feed them together, and play with them. We were doing all the things we had dreamed about together, having children, living in suburbia, building careers, and developing wonderful friendships. Our dreams were coming true.

After the divorce, I was in a daze for about a year, almost sleepwalking through life. The tensions in the house, the haggling over the agreement, his moving out, all of this was hard on everyone, probably the most difficult for the children. But it was the children who helped pull me out of that daze.

That first summer I got a job at a summer camp with no salary but free tuition for the children. It was a turning point. No one knew me there. I wasn't a failure. I was in a new world holding my own.

The change was also good for Marian and Steve; the good times at summer camp overshadowed the nightmare of the last year. It was harder for Beth. She was too young to sleep in a bunk and, after one week, ended up sleeping in my room. But we managed and came home renewed. I found work and began to remake my life.

I also quickly learned some of the skills of single parenting. Humor helped. Sometimes one or the other would say, "How come Stephen (or Marian or Beth) could do that."

I would answer with a laugh, "Because he (or she) is my favorite child." And everyone would chuckle.

I did my best to give the children a "normal" childhood on my own.

The next several summers we went on long camping trips, once for almost three weeks. Everyone thought I was either stupid or crazy; how could a woman with three small children go camping by herself, particularly since I had never camped before? But I had no money, how else could we go on a vacation?

I found a rental camping office that showed Stephen, my nine-year-old son, how to set up a tent. We also rented some lamps and pots, borrowed sleeping bags, and off we went. I wondered why everyone thought it was so difficult. It wasn't.

What was difficult was being alone with three children and no other adult to speak to. It reminded me of those early housebound days with sick children and the lonely days after the divorce. After that first camping experience, I always made sure there was another adult or family with us. By then, I knew other single parent households, we weren't such an oddity. And I had someone to talk to besides the children.

We had wonderful times on those camping trips, once traveling twelve hundred miles. More than just fun and adventure, those trips consolidated us as a family, a different family to be sure, but a family.

When I began the camping trips, friends would often ask, "What are you doing going alone," or "You never went camping before." These trips gave me the confidence to know that I could try new experiences; I didn't have to buy the myths of what I could and could not do. I could find out for myself.

There doesn't seem to be any apparent logic for why some memories reappear from time to time, some fade, never to be retrieved, and still others are strong and vivid. And the images of the children at different stages of life crop up at the strangest times.

Marian

Marian was always the force of life. Gurgling, laughing out loud, crawling, her vitality was always present, to touch, and to savor. The image of Marian at a party for one-year-olds is still so clear, it seems as if it were yesterday. She seemed the central presence, crawling with a wide smile, her eyes shining, claiming our attention and our conversation.

Marian attracted boys almost before she could walk. I never could put my finger on this extraordinary appeal she had. Boys were always there, calling on the telephone, ringing the bell, languishing on the living room couch waiting for Marian. While in Philadelphia in undergraduate school, she had to be hospitalized for an internal infection. I came to visit, and men of all ages—doctors, married and single students, friends, heads of departments—popped into the room to see Marian.

For a short time she dropped out of college and wandered to Alaska, worked in a fish factory in Gloucester, Massachusetts, and drove to the Midwest by herself. She always exuded confidence, told me not to worry, she was finding herself. Of course I worried anyhow. Finally, she did find herself, in science, in work, in marriage. She discovered her strong interest in science working at an animal hospital in Boston, where she met George.

Their children are confident, vital, passionate, and also exhilarated with the force of life. Now adults, her sons Todd and Justin are both working in jobs they love and leading productive lives.

In the last few years, Marian and George have taken up ballroom dancing, and sometimes I watch a particular video again. There is Marian, still slim, in her elegant, ball gowns dancing magically with her husband. George is a veterinarian and Marian an epidemiologist, and they both work long hours. It is a joy to see them dancing, a hobby so different from their working life. I always loved to dance and watching them brings me back to my own dancing days.

Stephen

When Stephen was a baby, he would drink his night bottle in his crib and we would close the door and wait. When we heard a loud thud we would know he had finished the bottle and thrown it out of the crib. From the beginning, Stephen was self-reliant, independent, and in charge of himself.

Stephen had trouble in first grade learning to read, it turned out he had dyslexia. The teachers who worked with him said he could read but needed to prove it for himself. When he was in fifth grade we were at my sister Milly's watching the film, *The Diary of Ann Frank.* After the film, he asked my sister if she had the book. She did, and he has been reading ever since. He reads more than any other adult I know, including me.

When he was in college, Linda, his high school sweetheart, committed suicide by jumping in front of a train at the Great Neck Railroad Station. He came home, Marian and Beth came home too, but he was inconsolable. After the funeral, he went back to school. I visited him the next week. When he saw me, his pain was palpable and he held on to me for a very long time. Linda and he had been together all through high school and a year or two during the college years. I was glad I understood that my grown son needed support and physical love and care.

Stephen was a science prodigy but after one semester in college he declared "I never want to be in a lab again in my life."

He changed his major to English literature. When he made up his mind, that was it. Steve often surprised me but I admired these qualities. Mysteriously, he had a sense of himself that belied his young years, and I knew enough, I don't know how I knew, to let him be.

One year he took a leave from college and worked in Boston in an institution for severely handicapped, disabled children. He always remembered them, what he learned, how they knew how to communicate. Another summer he was an automobile mechanic. He ended that summer with "I am going back to college, I don't want to see life looking up at the bottom of a car." After college and a few years at different jobs, he decided to become an attorney.

What I remember most vividly about Stephen is when he would come home periodically from law school, and the whole house would smell of cigarettes. There were match books everywhere, ashtrays stuffed with crumpled cigarette butts, *New Yorker* magazines piled high in the living room, orange peels in every basket. I would find one jogging shoe under the table and the other in the bathroom. Books were everywhere, to browse through and never put away.

He would come home with his lawyer briefs, and new resume, leave the tennis racket on the floor, the school clothes hung against the smart suits in the hall closet. He would come home, linger for a moment, and I would chuckle at his messiness, revel in his humor, sometimes hold out my hand and touch his hair.

I remember Steve with his long ponytail, his cowboy boots, his laid-back gentle ways, and his hamsters that drove us crazy all night. He always seems to know the best editor on the op-ed page, who wrote what, the height of every Celtic player, whether I should buy another chair, what happened to the Second Avenue subway.

Energetic, he is married to Anne, working hard, successful, and the father of Megan, Jonathan, and Michael, all independent, making their own lives. Stephen looks just like his father, and often I am startled when I see him. Charly and I divorced in the late 1960's. Steve is always a reminder of that earlier time—but I don't mind.

Beth

When Beth was a baby, Charly and I were supposed to take turns getting up at night to feed her. But we were so entranced with our new daughter that we both got up, one feeding her and the other watching.

In high school she managed a Carvel ice cream store, and every day she would ask in the morning, "Shall I bring ice-cream home?"

"No," we would answer, mindful of our calories. Before leaving for the night, she would call again, and we always gave in, eating ice-cream was our family fun, and how lucky we had Beth to supply it.

I think Beth surprises me the most—who she is, how she turned out, and the values she holds. To me she was the baby of the family. But even in high school, she managed the ice cream store. She was always resourceful and remarkable about finding her way.

Beth is five years younger than Steve and when Marian and Steve went off to college while she was still at home, she had the loneliest experience.

After college and some years working, she decided to get a Master's in Public Administration at Columbia. She was hired from this program to be the New York Governor's representative in the largest democratic county in New York, Brooklyn. She was a shining light, and has been ever since in whatever she tries.

She took up biking in New York. The year I was working in Israel, she sent me a picture of my car with eight bicycles on it, four on the roof and four on the trunk. "We don't want it to get stale, Mom." After working in New York for ten years, she went on a bike odyssey across the U.S. for four months, while deciding what to do next. She was tired of New York. Periodically, she called home, telling me where she was, what she had seen, what she endured. I, the anxious mother, would wait for those calls with both delight and trepidation. I was so proud of her courage, and her interest in exploring new experiences, whether it was nature, living style, or geography.

After her bike odyssey, she moved to Boston where Marian and Steve lived, met her husband, John, and has one son, Jake, who was born in 1996. Before her wedding she took me to an AMC camp in New Hampshire to share her love of hiking and the mountains. In her short stay in Boston, she hiked eighty percent of the trails.

Several years ago, she and I went to Key West and Miami Beach. What fun we had exploring the restaurants, the musical shows in Key West, the shops in Miami. She did the driving and made arrangements for where we would stay, how we could get there, what we would do. It was a real reversal of roles and an extreme pleasure.

Her life, however, has been the most difficult; John was very ill for one long year with the flesh eating disease, Necrotizing Fasciitis. They lost their business and their home years later. But they rebuilt their lives with courage and determination. I marvel at their amazing resiliency. And Beth is still adventurous, hiking, biking, and experimenting with new work roles. Jake has inherited this spirit.

The Feast

I often think about those long-ago days of mothering. I want to capture it all again, tie a shoe, cuddle a child, kiss a cheek. When they were young, they used to complain, "You're not listening." And now I try to listen all the time, to who they are, human, loving, complex.

For me there is always something of a mystery about the children and how they turned out. How come they are all such good cooks with different styles of cooking? Why did all three intermarry? How did these products of the 60's, the flower children, the experimenters with drugs, with sex, with life styles, learn to be such tender, wonderful parents? They ended up liking themselves, liking each other, and liking me.

I feast my eyes on my children, grown, beautiful, building an order to their lives, having their own children. I feast my eyes on the richness of the harvest and the miracle of it all.

7

Thanksgiving Feast

I feast my eyes on the children
my children
grown, beautiful
building an order to their lives.

My eldest getting married
to a wonderful young man
Another in law school,
not quite together yet about his life,
his vocation, his love,
But together in his head, his vitality
his assessment of things.

And the youngest
when did she get so lovely,
so tall, so slim,
so elegant,
getting off the train
hugging her brother.

I feast my eyes on my nieces and nephews
growing up, getting taller,

building an order to their lives.
Carrying the chairs, setting the table,
laughing as I torture the turkey.

I feast my eyes on the richness of the
harvest, of young people
having birthdays, arguing about politics,
growing older, entering adulthood.

I feast my eyes
on the miracle of it all.

8

The Sweater

Sometimes when I'm cold, I wear the sweater I bought for my mother a long time ago. I slip my arms into the long sleeves, wrap the sweater around me, and imagine my mother is giving me a hug.

The sweater is beige and bulky with rows of cable stitching down each side. I bought it at Bloomingdales, one of the boutique department stores in New York, as a birthday present for her. At the time, it was an extravagant gift for me—working on a professor's salary, living in a wonderful, but broken-down house that needed repairs, and raising three children as a single parent.

I doubt if she ever wore the sweater. She never wore the presents any of us gave her, especially those from my father. He could not please her. I cringed when he brought her a present, and she would find some way to make him take it back. I felt myself screaming a long, slow, silent scream, "like it, like it, like it, make him feel good." But she couldn't, she could not give any of us the pleasure of liking the gifts we bought her.

I don't remember ever getting a hug from my mother. Sometimes, she put her lips to a cheek, a quick peck, but it didn't mean anything. Perhaps her inability to be affectionate was a generational style, I don't know, but this characteristic was also an accurate reflection of my mother's personality.

She had a propensity for holding on to anger, sulking, never letting go, whether the anger was directed at something trivial or important, whether it came from an issue from yesterday or ten years ago, or whether it was based on reality or her imagination. Anger was anger, and she could not distinguish between causes and solutions.

Yet, she was very sociable and had a wonderful gift for hospitality. All my childhood years, I remember family dinners, special feasts, friends of my parents, our friends, congregating at our house. Everyone was always welcome. As a hostess, she was gracious, generous, funny, and warm. As a mother, she was cold, remote, and intrusive. My sister, Milly, once said, "It would be much better for us if Mom treated us as guests rather than as her children."

Once she did say that her heart was filled with love for me. That was in 1980, the time I traveled to Florida to plead for family peace at my daughter, Marian's wedding that coming May. Marian wanted assurance that my mother would not make a scene with her father, my former husband, at her wedding. Charly and my mother once had a dispute about ownership of her stocks which she never forgot. It was decided in her favor in a courtroom. She was also angry at his treatment of me before and after the divorce. Even though she had just declared her love, the only time I remember she did that, she was outraged at the request, and screamed all kinds of insults. Her love could change in an instant to rage, but she did behave at the wedding, sulking part of the time, but eventually enjoying herself.

When she wasn't angry, she looked beautiful. She had the high cheekbones of the women of her family, her mother and her aunts, which I inherited.

Her eyes were a penetrating hazel, sometimes almost green. My eyes were brown, or so it said on my driver's license. One day in Jerusalem, a colleague remarked one day, "You have the most beautiful, penetrating, hazel eyes."

"No," I replied, "my eyes are brown."

"Look into the mirror," she said.

My eyes *were indeed* hazel. Was this some mystical force, a legacy from my mother who died the day before I left for Israel for a year to direct a college program? In Jerusalem, I could believe in the magic of such transformations. On my return to the United States, the ophthalmologist tried to squash fantasies about magic and mystical happenings. He explained that as the cornea gets older the eye color can change. Let him think what he will. I do have my mother's hazel eyes now, and he cannot dispute the cheekbones.

Although my mother—her name was Ida—believed in education, she was also confused about what she wanted for her daughters.

"Don't let boys know how smart you are," she warned my sister and me. "You will never get married if you do."

For a long time, I did think my intelligence was some kind of curse. She bragged about my achievements publicly, but in front of me she scorned the doctorate.

"You are a workaholic and what can you really cure?"

She was the middle child with an older sister and a younger brother. Her parents were immigrants from Russia. Her brother was their favorite child. He was given meat each day for dinner while the girls were fed leftovers. No matter how strong or powerful she might seem to her children and husband, she suffered from feelings of inferiority that began in childhood.

I am the eldest of four children. My sister, Milly, was born sixteen months after me, my brother Marvin came four years after that.

I can still hear my father shouting for joy when Marvin was born. "It's a boy, it's a boy. Finally, we have a boy."

My second brother, Samuel, was born seven years later.

My mother had a real mean streak. She gave away my brother, Marvin's dog when he was in school. She told him the dog wandered away. Marvin, just ten at the time, searched the neighborhood for months.

After she and my father separated, she tortured my younger brother, Samuel, every time he went to see our father. She wanted total loyalty as a symbol of our love, not understanding the devastating effect it had on all of us, but most critically on my already emotionally fragile, younger brother.

Once, she told me she was cutting me out of her will, I could make my own way, but I objected strenuously, and she changed it back.

She had a "cat of nine tails." She threatened us with it often, but I don't remember her ever using it.

She hated our independence, but if we were in need, she was there. She helped me with my dental bills and my children's shoes, bought me a new car when my husband took mine during the divorce proceedings, paid for some of my son Stephen's law school tuition, and took care of the children when I needed to attend professional meetings for a few days.

She was gutsy. She learned to drive in the early forties—an old Graham with a clutch—when few woman her age drove. My mother and father had a long court battle over the financial aspects of divorce. When my father left her with no money, she got a job as a bookkeeper, knowing nothing about bookkeeping. A friend who was experienced at that line of work helped her at lunch and after work.

The unpredictability of my parents' lives together had us always on edge—one day all love and kisses, the next, my father was punching her on the kitchen floor or she was calling the police for one of his numerous infractions such as playing cards, going to the racetrack, bringing home ham. I spent many nights crying in my bed, thinking about how I might patch things up between my parents.

Everyone thought we were the ideal family. My parents managed to have four children together, he was a successful entrepreneur, a young self-educated man from the Lower East Side, and we had lots of material things. We had lessons of all kinds, household help, and a second home in the country. From the outside it did look wonderful. For me now, it is difficult to understand how they stayed married for so long.

I think my father finally wanted peace, he could not stand the constant conflict.

She was always in a love-hate relationship with my father even after he left her and lived with another woman. She insisted we walk down the aisle with her at his funeral—she treated it like a wedding rather than a funeral.

After she married her second husband, Jack, who was quite mad, she lived six months of the year in Florida and six months of the year in Montreal. His permanent residence was in Canada and all his children and grandchildren lived there.

While driving in the car I would write my mother letters by audio taping. Sometimes she responded. I still have those tapes, but only once in all these years could I play one. The sound of her voice is still too much for me to hear. I don't know why.

I never think of a clinical label to fit my mother. Probably today, she would be given some drug and be able to live a somewhat normal life. In fact, in those last days, dying in a hospital in Montreal, she was on some drug that made her a totally different person, calm, open, amiable, and rational.

My mother believed that a lady wore white gloves when she

went out of the house and that a good wife always had neat bureau drawers. She inspected mine whenever she visited. I never questioned her right to invade my privacy. She was committed to education, and we had every kind of lesson you can imagine: piano, elocution, horseback-riding, typing, shorthand, and Hebrew. A college education was a given; we never expected anything else. Yet she was totally intimidated by our education and achievements.

My mother was persistent about growing vegetables, particularly corn. She measured the height of the corn weekly. For two summers in a row she tried to grow watermelon, but they never ripened.

Milk chocolate was one of her favorite snacks, particularly the thick Hershey bars made up of squares. She kept the bars in the refrigerator eating only two squares each night before going to bed. She loved beautiful things, particularly English china, and she had a huge collection of cups and saucers from England. Some of those cups and her "good" dishes are now in my daughter Beth's home, lined up in a glass-fronted, antique cabinet in the dining room. My mother would rejoice with that cabinet and its prominent place where everyone could see these acquisitions. Every time I look at this cabinet I am jolted by memories of the arguments about her antique purchases—my father vehemently disapproved of spending money on things that "break so easily."

She would squirrel away things. Once she hid $14 in quarters in my house when she came to visit. Every time she came she searched for those quarters but never could find them. Many years later when I sold the house and we were cleaning up to move, Stephen found the quarters hidden in the bottom of a large drawer in the dining room. Finally, we figured out why it was so difficult to close that drawer. Stephen called my mother claiming "finders, keepers," and even she laughed.

She loved her grandchildren, particularly when they were babies.

When a new baby was born, she came from wherever she was to help. When my daughter, Marian, had her first child she came to visit from Montreal. One day when the three of us went to the supermarket, she stopped everyone, almost to our embarrassment, to have them take notice, "we are four generations here."

Most of all she loved us, her children. Although she had a funny way, often destructive way, of showing it, we were the center of her life. She taught me many things—that mothering, with all its difficulties, was wonderful. Many of her attitudes I did not want to emulate. Because she made it so difficult for us to love our father, I learned to make it easy for my own children, to help them through the divorce, to remember their father's birthday, to know that their affection for him did not take anything away from me. She didn't intend to teach me what I didn't have growing up, but through my own experience I learned what I needed and what my children needed—satisfying work, family, curiosity, and a desire to stretch the imagination. And she was the one who taught me how to be resourceful.

When and how does the fear of a parent begin to change to forgiveness, understanding, and maybe love, however tentative? All the anger and bitterness I felt from and for her as a child and young adult somehow dissolved with time. Why? How? There is so much in life that is a mystery that cannot be anticipated or explained. What is the mystery of this bond between mother and daughter, this bond of both separateness and connection? Perhaps in my own development as an adult, I became more aware of her deep and buried loneliness and the frustration of her unused intelligence. As I resolved my own inner demons, I began to develop empathy for her fears and feelings of inadequacy.

This woman who tyrannized us when we were young was really powerless, the victim of her own myths, taboos, and belief in conformity and convention. She did not have the tools to reflect on her inner conflicts, to understand her lack of resolution and why the middle-class, immigrant dream of living happily ever after in America could not always be fulfilled. She was a product of another time, a generation that had no knowledge of the feminist movement central to my own development.

I cannot pinpoint the moment in time when my feelings for her changed. Slowly, as I began to have more insight into who she was and why, I began to feel connected even through her anger. Time washed away the bitterness.

Now, sometimes alone at night, or late in the afternoon coming home from a busy day, I want to call her up and say "Hello." I don't have anything special in mind, just a strong longing to recapture all those days of both love and loveless times, of connection, of our family. She died in 1987, on July 18th, the day of my granddaughter's first birthday, the day before I was to leave for Israel for a year. Sometimes when I feel wistful or cold or lonely, I wear her sweater and fold the sleeves around me like a giant hug from another planet.

9

Generations

When I look into the mirror now
I see my mother's face,
the glimpse startles me,
I am uneasy with the brush of time.
Are we shadows of each other?

From the cradle of her time,
the bitterness eludes me
I feel her kindness,
her lovingness flowing
out to me and mine.

10

Who Talked to Him Last?

The most lasting memory I have of my father was his funeral, and now, fifty years later, the image of him in his casket is still vivid and strong. My mother sat on one side of the aisle and the "other woman," (her name was Jean) on the other. My mother was trying to impress everyone with the idea that he really loved her. Probably, she was really trying to convince herself. My three siblings and I were hoping and praying that there would not be any scenes and were so nervous and tense we had no energy to think about grieving or to feel the loss.

My mother and father separated about ten years before he died. My father told me he was leaving my mother as he danced with me at my wedding. They never formally divorced—he never offered her enough money—in fact, they made the law journals; their case was so long and bizarre. But he "married" Jean in another state, and, although he was not legally free to marry, he introduced her as his wife.

My father died in 1961 from lung cancer. He was fifty-seven.

In the early 60's we were surprised when someone died from lung cancer. Smoking was not yet publicly tied to cancer. All his adult life he smoked at least three packs a day—Camels and Chesterfield were his favorites. Filtered cigarettes were rarely sold in those days and, even if they were, he would never smoke them. Denial about any aspect of his body and health was a strong force in his personality.

During the three weeks preceding his death, I came to see him every day. He was a patient at New York Hospital in New York City. How I managed to come into New York everyday from the suburbs with three young children is still a mystery to me. And why? I had such a fragile relationship with him. What was that compulsion about? To get to know him? To forgive him? Each day, as he began to recover from the surgery, I stayed a little longer.

On the day of the surgery, my husband, Charly, Jean, and I walked around the city for five hours while the surgery was in process. Jean, a younger version of my mother, did not seem as neurotic, or so it appeared that day. It was the first time I spent more than a few minutes with her. We were never invited to the "wedding" or to any events at their home. I didn't meet her daughter until the day of my father's funeral even though she was young and lived with them. My mother called her the witch. How often the other woman is blamed for the husband's adultery!

My father's name was Nathan. He came to this country with his parents and younger sister when he was two years old. At Ellis Island they asked my grandmother when he was born. She said Passover. His birthday became March 21st, the first day of Spring. Our dismay about his will was compounded by the mystery of his birth. When was he really born? Who was he really?

My father's parents were uneducated people from some remote village in Russia. They settled in the Lower East Side of New York, and my grandfather opened a small shoe store. He sold and fixed shoes. My only memory of him is in this store wearing a dirty apron and fixing shoes. He also died in his fifties.

My grandmother was a very tall, heavy woman with breasts down to her stomach. When she stayed at our house I couldn't help but stare at those huge breasts. She had long gray hair which she brushed morning and night and wore in a bun. She was in this country for thirty years and the only two English words she knew were okay and goodbye. She loved movies and often would take my sister and me on Saturday afternoons. I have no idea what she did and did not understand. When my grandmother died, there was nothing from her past. No papers, no pictures, only a few vases she brought from Europe.

When my father was young, my grandmother would often come to his school unannounced, go into the class, and yell loudly at the teacher. Nobody knew what she was excited about because she spoke only Yiddish. My father told us how embarrassed he was, but there was nothing he could do to stop her.

My father was in the sausage-casing business. He had a plant on 138th Street next to the 3rd Ave. El. It was a large place with offices in front and a factory in the back. Men in high boots stood around raised platforms washing and filling the casings. The working space had to be kept cold and damp to keep the casings fresh. I still remember the dampness. My father had bought the last shipment of casings from South America just before the Second World War. At that time, it was a financial coup. He did have an instinct for making money and also exuded confidence about his business success, particularly after the profits from South America came rolling in.

The contradiction between his workplace and his fastidious personal style was startling. He was a "dapper dresser," clean, well-shaven, black hair combed straight back across his head.

His business was successful, but he tortured my mother by

bringing home non-kosher meats, sausage and ham. She made him eat these foods in the basement.

My mother's sister and brother both worked for him for long periods of time. He tortured them too, but it was during the depression era and they needed jobs. Many years after my father died, my aunt told me that she knew about all his womanizing, but couldn't tell my mother.

After he separated from my mother and before he joined with Jean, he lived by himself in a brand-new building in an elegant section of the Bronx. I visited him there once. He was sitting in a beautiful smoking jacket, something right out of the movies. It was the smoking jacket I bought for him from my first paycheck. The boy who grew up in poverty on the Lower East Side loved the grander side of life, the smoking jackets, the big cars, the expensive restaurants. He always had the biggest car on the block, trading it in every two years.

During my childhood we lived very well. My mother had household help. We lived in a big house in the West Bronx and had a series of summer homes. Our home was the center for all our friends. My parents were wonderful hosts, and our friends were always welcome. My affable father was a social dynamo, making jokes, telling women "if only I had seen you first." We discovered much later that he had a long-standing affair with my Aunt Rose, my mother's childhood friend, who was like a member of our family.

My father loved to gamble at cards and the race track. Pinochle and gin rummy were his games. He frequented the horse races, particularly the trotters in Yonkers. He once confided to me that he used one of the tellers there who always told him what to bet in return for a $50 dollar bill. He loved liquor, scotch and water was his favorite. He loved food, and gambling, the "good things of life." and any acquisitions that took him far away from the Lower East Side.

He often told us stories about his growing up. I remember once there was an announcement on the radio that some man was going to be electrocuted in Sing Sing. My father said he knew him, that they had grown up together.

"All my friends," he said, "either died in the electric chair or became successful businessmen and it was difficult to distinguish between the two."

My father was always seeing a psychiatrist. Sometimes we had to visit the office of the present one to be queried about life at home. Once he brought someone home to dinner, a Dr. Benson,, who told us to chew each bite twenty-two times for the food to be digested. We were all intimidated, chewing away and trying to count. The meal was interminable.

I did not have anything concrete of my father. My sister had some pictures of him, a picture of him at his Bar Mitzvah, sitting on a bench reading, pictures of him with us and our mother, the perfect family, on a trip. After my sister died, I took all the pictures and sometimes I just stare at them; I am always surprised at what he really looked like. Is this my father? He is a stranger and familiar at the same time.

There were parts of my father that I loved and admired. You could always depend on him in an emergency or crisis. When someone in our family needed an abortion—abortions were illegal then—he knew just where to go, took her, and paid the bills. If someone needed a job, he would help by calling all his friends. He had a huge network, mainly from his childhood, people who had all become successful. During the early part of the Second World War, he sponsored many Jewish people to come to this country.

And he was fun. He had a hearty laugh, loved to tell jokes and carry out pranks. He was as much engaged in the radio programs as we were—the Lone Ranger and the Shadow. He loved theater, and often took the whole family out to dinner and the theater. He also loved to eat, and I remember those gigantic meals we used to have on City Island, everything from steamed clams to a special apple pie. On Friday nights when he came home to our house in the country after his week in the city, he would honk his horn three times at the top of the long hill near our home. We would run out with glee, jumping and kissing him. He knew how to drive the car fast over the top of a hill to give us a sense of a surge as we yelled "whoopee."

My father was a reader. He introduced us to all the great literature of the time and particularly novels with a socialist theme. Upton Sinclair was one of his favorites. When Dewey ran for governor in New York State, he told me he was going to vote for him. I couldn't believe it. Once he had money, he gave up his political convictions. He was fundamentally pragmatic and an opportunist.

Despite all his bravado, he was fearful. Mostly he was afraid of death, and now, after all these years, I wonder how he felt those weeks in the hospital before he died.

My father believed that his daughters should always have a way of making a living. He had a man come to our house to teach my sister and me steno and typing. That was his vision for us—we could become secretaries.

Years later, my sister was Phi Beta Kappa, and I have a doctorate, but he was ahead of his time, and steno and typing came in handy all through our lives.

My mother and father had a love-hate relationship. Sometimes, even for weeks on end, there was an idyllic feeling in the home. Then suddenly out of nowhere, she would be on the floor, threatening to call the police as he was pummeling her with his fists. We never understood or could anticipate where these fights came from. Usually, if a fight was to begin, it was at the dinner table when we were all together.

They were fiercely competitive about our love for them, suggesting if we loved the other we were disloyal. They wanted us to love only one of them at a time. It was a difficult way to grow up. Sometimes he would love us intensely, buy us fur coats and all sorts of treats. Other times he was completely indifferent to us, not knowing what grade we were in or seeming to care.

Several days after my father's funeral, we went to his lawyer's office—my mother and sister, my two brothers, my husband and I—for the reading of the will. My father was a fairly wealthy man. According to New York State law, he had to leave one-third of his estate to my mother. He left her the interest on one third and the principal was to come to us when she died. She was penniless, and we gave her the entire amount.

Except for a few minor bequests to us, everything was left to Jean. Her brother was the executor of the will. We should have anticipated that he would leave everything to her. Whoever got to him last was the person he believed. The most difficult part about the will was accepting the fact that he didn't really care for us, did not know what we were doing and how we were each struggling.

While my parents were living together, everything was in his name, he gave my mother an "allowance" and one of their running arguments was how she needed an increase. I think she took money from his pockets when he was asleep. Sometimes she would buy something with a credit card and then return the item to keep the money.

My father is buried someplace in New Jersey. I don't even know the name of the cemetery and have not been there since the funeral. The total omission of his own family left nothing for us to grieve, to want to remember, to go back to the cemetery to mourn. If we mourned at all, it was for what should have been, for what fathers leave to children, for how fathers care for children. How could we mourn?

How does one grieve? I tried going back to the scenes of my father and our family. The section of Manhattan where my father grew up does not exist in that shape anymore; it became Soho and artists and restaurants are there now. The section of the Bronx, where I grew up, is now an urban slum. I once went to visit our summer house; it seemed so small compared to my memory of its greatness.

How can you sum up a life? Every life has its contradictions, but his contradictions seemed more dramatic and inexplicable. A man who grew up poor on the Lower East Side, a successful businessman, a gambler, a womanizer, a person with few ethical standards, a charmer with a great sense of humor. I sometimes yearn to grasp the mystery and essence of my father. To finally grieve, perhaps, for the father who never existed. But how? And why?

11

Mourning

The contentment and family solidarity that I tried to cultivate for my children had to be molded around periods of mourning, the loss of what our family had been as well as the deaths of five people close to us who died while we lived in our house.

My children and I mourned the death of the marriage for a very long time. After the divorce I remember the sadness I felt as I watched my children feeling wistful at a school function, out to dinner, at a movie and at Little League baseball games. My son stared at fathers and sons. Whatever else I could accomplish, I could not be the father at the baseball game or the Cub Scouts. The sadness that comes from the death of a marriage, the mourning for what was and what might have been, envelops the entire family.

Although I always knew that mourning is a part of life, I began to realize that I needed to help my children cope with their sadness so that they could still find joy.

Truthfully, I cannot really recall how my children emerged from the initial shock of the separation. Although I did my best not to express anger at their father, I was struggling, as they were, with the complexities of divorce. I had new responsibilities for which I was not prepared. I tried as best I could to help my children.

Time does help, and developing a new family structure slowly provided strength. At the beginning the children were hesitant about their father's visiting schedule and would leave the house hesitantly to get into his car. As the new-style family mode became part of the weekly routine, it became easier. Bringing other single families to the house for dinner or family excursions, integrating the children into my social life, and the camping trips reinforced the idea that yes, "we were a family."

One of my son's friends said to me one day, "My family is going through what your family had to."

"What is that," I replied.

"Divorce," he answered quietly.

I realized then that my children's friends talked about what was going on in each family, and did, I hoped, help each other. I also understood why and how Steve's friend needed to talk to me because his parents were going through such difficulty at that time.

*

Five people died while we lived in our house. There were years between each one. But it is still difficult to remember now how we as a family dealt with these individual deaths. They were painful times and I tried as best as I could to talk about each person with my children.

I grew up at a time when children were protected from death; it was never talked about. I did not have any experience, and probably, as I think about those times now, I wonder could I have done more to help my children?

My father was the first. He died three years before we were

divorced. He was only fifty-seven when he died from lung cancer and surgery. He left little, no heritage, ideas, values, only the fantasy or wish of what might have been if he had been different, if his life had been different. Even his money he left to someone else with few provisions for his children.

My children were young when he died, and though my relationship with him was complex and distant, they had a different image. He had been a regular visitor to our home when my brother, Sam lived with us. We spent many hours talking about what fun they had with my father, and the presents he gave them.

*

One of the most troubling deaths was my brother, Sam, the youngest in our family, and thirteen years my junior. He had been troubled for a very long time, and at fifteen tried to kill himself. He spent several months in a mental hospital (those existed at that time) and when he was ready to leave, the psychiatrists believed he could not live with either of my parents. They were not capable.

After much discussion, he came to live with my family and me. It was difficult at first, and my ex-husband was very helpful in dealing with the problems. Sometimes Sam would not get up for three days at a time. But gradually he improved, went to high school and made friends. Sam was part of our family.

Sam dropped out of high school three months before his graduation. He just could not allow himself to be successful. After my father died, he went back to live with my mother and began working at the airport. Soon after, he became engaged to be married. In retrospect he was trying to replicate all the life issues his friends were experiencing, work and marriage, but apparently, he could not find peace with his sense of hopelessness. It is possible that one of the reasons for his desperation was the debts he owed at the local bridge club where he played for money. He owed $1,000, not a hefty sum even in those days, but an impossible obstacle for a troubled young man.

I often wondered if he felt trapped in his engagement. He really did not want to marry that young woman, but he always needed some semblance of normality for reassurance that he was leading a constructive life.

I spoke to him the evening before he committed suicide. I asked to see him the next day. He said, "I can't, I have something to do." Sam had bought a long hose at Sears and Roebuck and killed himself in a closed garage when he was just twenty-one years old.

I was angry for a very long time. We had tried to help him in so many ways, and it was all for naught. My mother was inconsolable. I can't remember how my children experienced his death, perhaps because I was in such a state of shock. He had lived with us, played with them. But I didn't talk about it for many years and only recently placed a picture of him on the bookcase with other family pictures.

*

Only fifty-five, my friend, Lillian, died suddenly of a heart attack. I was in my early forties, and my children were young. Her loss was hard for all of us.

Lillian had been very much a part of all our lives. The image that keeps surfacing is that night many years ago when we had a hurricane and the lights went out. In the middle of the storm, there was a knock at the door, and there was Lillian wearing her big bear coat and heavy boots. She barged in, laughing and shouting to all of us, "Let's all sleep in front of the fire."

Lillian had accurately guessed how frightened I might be alone in the house with three young children, with the storm and candles. That night, the five of us, bundled in blankets, curled up in front of the fire's glow, and fell asleep. What began as frightening ended up as fun. What a wonderful image of closeness and connectedness, love and sensitivity.

Lillian befriended me at the time of the divorce. She was fifteen years older than I and the director of our local, cooperative nursery school. That was the setting for our evolving friendship. She had extraordinary insight into children's lives, their difficulties and strengths. Her own marriage was a shambles, but for me she was pure delight.

She took me to New York often to see the big city, "to get a slice of life," she would say. She had a fondness for gay bars, places I had never been to before. Gradually, I began to understand if she lived just a few years later, she would have been able to explore her sexual identity, quite different from the masquerade she endured for most of her adult life. She helped me through the most difficult passage of my life, my divorce, and I still miss her.

Her death was not easy for any of us. She exuded such a strong life force, was a vital presence in our home, came often to dinners and Passover Seders. Young as they were, my children came to her funeral, they needed to express their own grief.

*

Those losses could not quite prepare us, however, for the suicide of Linda, Stephen's high school girl friend. She was bright, productive, interesting, and had a great sense of humor. In high school, she had a fellowship to go abroad for a semester, an unusual experience for a high school student. She was a member of our household, and everyone in the family loved her.

Everything changed during the college years. I don't know how to describe it, but she simply could not find herself and what she wanted to do. When everyone started going to college, she just dropped out, and dropped out further and further and found it harder and harder to get back.

Stephen and Linda had been a couple for three years during high school. She was planning to go to Boston to live with my older daughter, Marian. Everyone thought a new setting with young people might be an answer for her.

Instead, one day she jumped in front of a train at the Great Neck Railroad station. My son was changed forever. The death of someone so young and so close to him gave him an uncanny understanding of the randomness of life and how people needed to be cherished.

Like my brother, Sam, she was consumed with hopelessness so profound that it is difficult for me to even imagine. Stephen, Marian, and Beth all came home for the funeral; we all mourned her death for a very long time. Stephen was inconsolable for two weeks, then one day awoke and said, "I need to get back to school." I visited him several times at school, and we talked about Linda and what they had done together.

*

It was a sudden and unexpected illness that caused the death of Nancy, my friend Sheila's daughter. Sheila and I both worked at the same unit of the State University of New York. We worked with students on Long Island and traveled upstate together several times a month. Long car rides lead to intimate conversations, and we became very close friends.

Nancy was Sheila's oldest child. At twenty-seven, she was already an established screen and television writer, living in Hollywood. She had almost completed a book about the Hollywood witch hunt during the McCarthy days, *The Hollywood Writers' Wars*, which was published after her death.

She was in New York working and met Sheila and me for dinner.

She complained of a headache, and we told her to see a doctor when she returned home to Los Angeles. Within twenty-four hours after the visit to the doctor, she was in a hospital to surgically remove a brain tumor. Two weeks later, her brain stem was severely damaged, and she went into a coma, was placed on a ventilator, and died two weeks later.

I went to the funeral in California and again a month later to revisit with Sheila all the places Nancy lived, worked, and played. During that visit, I learned more about friendship, and what it means to help someone in great need. I was beginning to fully comprehend how the random acts of life can affect any of us.

Three of the people who died while we lived in our house were in their twenties, and Lillian was forever young. As I write about these experiences today, I wonder how with all these deaths and the mourning that followed, we managed to live our lives with energy, hope, and creativity. I must have intuitively helped my children and myself through these experiences, but I don't remember how.

Perhaps, because our home was about youth, people growing up, my children growing up, me growing up, all of us young, finding our way, searching, exploring, questioning, and establishing our identities. Perhaps we survived because we learned in some way to embrace all the subtleties and life transformations—divorce, mourning, and laughter too.

12

Memories and Memorabilia

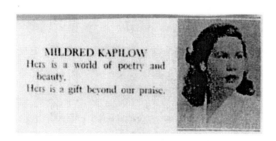

MILDRED KAPILOW
Hers is a world of poetry and beauty.
Hers is a gift beyond our praise.

Milly Kapilow
April 4th, 1928 –November 17th, 2008

What is a life? What is the particular journey, shape, hills, obstacles, and triumphs? My sister, Milly. died on November 17th, 2008. Her journey had all the hills, obstacles, and triumphs that every life might have. But somehow there was always something distinctive about Milly, and her life was carved out differently. For our generation she was unique in where and how she lived, what she did to earn money, her social life, and the gifts she gave to people she cared about.

Sometimes there was great drama and excitement, and at other times unrelenting sadness and tragedy. Contradiction was her password

Milly loved New York. She lived in a building on 8th Avenue between 54th and 55th Streets, which became my home away from home after I moved to Boston. Her story in that building is an ode to Milly, to New York, and to a slice of life repeated again and again in a million ways.

Warm, generous, and loving, she was a gracious hostess and welcomed me any time. As we grew older we found a special companionship and peace together. I miss her finishing touches for my writing.

She was sixteen months younger than I, the second in a family of four. In elementary school, my mother was asked to take Milly and me to Columbia University for testing. I don't remember what my intelligence score was, (somewhere in the 130's I think) but I remember hers—142, genius level. At that time you needed to take an exam to go to Hunter High School, my sister did and was accepted. She always said that was the best educational experience of her life.

Milly was Phi Beta Kappa with a major in English Literature. After graduation from college, she competed with twelve hundred women to get a job at KLM in Holland, and, after several years there moved to Australia, also working in advertising. In the United States, she was the administrator of the library division at Macmillan, the first woman to hold that post. For several years she administered her own consulting company and lived in a stunning brownstone on 12th Street. But her life turned bleak for a long time as her periods of creativity alternated with periods of depression and anxiety.

She never married. There were many men in her life, but she rejected marriage. She mothered my children in different ways, and her home in Greenwich Village was a thrill for them and their friends during the heyday of the sixties and seventies.

There was a long period when she would not go further than 12th St., but then her brownstone was sold and she had to move. After months of procrastination and years of drifting she finally moved to West 55th Street, and gradually over time, was renewed and rejoicing.

300 West 55th St. was built in 1962. My sister started off in a studio and, after several years, moved to a one-bedroom apartment. Her next-door neighbor had a music studio in his apartment. The noise and drums at all hours of the day and night were deafening. In desperation, she bought a pair of Chinese gongs and every time the music started she would bang on the gongs. This noise, too, was deafening, but the neighbors approved of anyone spunky enough to retaliate against the music studio.

Finally, she went to a Legal Aid attorney who told her to hold back the rent until the landlord did something about the music. The landlord did try but lost in court. Fortunately a two-bedroom apartment became available, and the landlord offered her the apartment if she would pay all the back rent. She moved to the 19th floor to a blissfully silent, lovely, two-bedroom apartment she converted into a bed and breakfast. She hosted guests from all over the world until the summer before she died.

She loved fairy tales, and her apartment was her own invented fairy tale with bed canopies, tassels, drapes, stuffed animals, dolls, and paintings on every possible empty wall space including the kitchen cabinets. The apartment was filled with memorabilia from her work and life in Holland and Australia, her travels, and thrift shops. She collected photographs from every branch of the family, which also adorned her walls and furniture.

Living on 8th Avenue and 55th Street, Milly could walk to everything that she loved.

Her wide circle of friends was family, and they all had subscriptions to the Metropolitan Opera, the Philharmonic, City Center, and Carnegie Hall. They were regulars at the Amato Opera Company in the Bowery and saw every new play. Milly was a devoted Yankee fan and knew every player and their batting averages. She viewed baseball as a wonderful ballet with music and choreography all its own.

You could live for years in my sister's building and never cross the street. That was perfect for Milly because she was a night owl, and often went shopping at the oddest hours. Everyone knew her in the combination food and drug store.

On the northern side of the entrance to her building were a liquor store, cleaner, shoe repair shop, luggage store, ice-cream store, and a fast food restaurant for soups and sandwiches. Two men from India ran the ice-cream store, which also housed an internet café. One of the men could barely speak English and did not know how to say the various flavors. Milly would often translate for him.

The doormen were Hispanic, African American, and Caucasian; gracious people, who remembered me even when I did not come for long periods of time. That is amazing to me since there are four hundred and one units in this building and lots of people coming and going. They probably remembered me because they loved Milly. She was a building character, and many of her neighbors came to see me when she died. There was the opera singer next door, the rental agent on the other side of her, Katherine who lived across the hall and cried in the elevator when I told her Milly died, the woman with two babies, and Elizabeth with her dog.

My sister loved dogs and once ran a course for the Learning Annex on how to live with a dog in New York. When Elizabeth traveled for work, she would leave her dog with Milly. Even after Milly's vision began to deteriorate and she could not dog-sit any longer, Elizabeth and her dog would come to visit.

Milly's passions were reading, the Times crossword puzzles, needlepoint, the cultural life of New York, and her many friends from all over the world. Most of the people who came to stay in her apartment became her friends and would come on a yearly basis. She had an enormous capacity for generosity, finding gifts for friends, relatives, and everyone else in mysterious places in the city.

When Milly died, I found wrapped and labeled Christmas gifts for neighbors. I had the honor and sorrow of distributing them.

During her last few years she suffered from macular degeneration and had to give up reading but resisted giving up her library. Using a huge magnifying lamp she continued her needlepoint and all kinds of puzzles. Milly never complained about either the loss of vision or the cancer from which she died. A week before her death she talked about how good her life had been. I was awed by her nobility and grace at this crisis.

She did not want anyone at her funeral that she did not know and I conducted the service. Everyone talked about their own memories. She had selected and marked the music she wished to be played, four songs by Strauss. They were labeled in a white envelope.

I drink my morning coffee out of Milly's mug, the one with the blue bird. I've worn her red gloves to the movies. The picture of her at a Yankee game hangs in my kitchen. Her embroidery covers two walls. Milly introduced me to the opera; it is one of her legacies to me. Now, I go on Saturday afternoons to one of these large theaters where they simultaneously show the opera as it is performed at the Met. I watch the people coming in, see the box where Milly and her friends sat. I know it is not possible, but I keep hoping I will see her.

I moved to Boston when I retired and realize that I am no longer a New Yorker, although many of the values of New York are still in my blood. Milly would be so pleased; I am still a Yankee fan.

By Milly Kapilow, her sampler, Fire Island. 1971

No Minutes Surely Bring Us More Content
Than these in Wholly Useless Hobbies Spent
So Silly Sewers Pass Fine Days & Hours
Embroidering Idiotic Leaves And Flowers
But Better Fingers Pricked & Vision Double
Then Pricks That Get Us Sewers Into Trouble

Milly, in her bedroom—Dressed for a masquerade.

13

The Waiting Room

My family and I are sitting on hard-backed chairs in the waiting room of a large hospital in downtown Boston. We are afraid to talk about what we are waiting for. We also do not want to disturb all the other people in this crowded room. The people here are too tired to talk anyhow. There is an air of expectancy mingled with acute anxiety in this room as everyone waits to hear the outcome of their loved one, good news or bad.

Nothing else seems to matter, except what is happening here, in the operating room or down the hall in the intensive care unit. Occasionally, someone turns on the television set and there is a glimpse of the outside world. That world outside this waiting room seems almost an intrusion, our minds are focused here, and this is where anything that is important is happening. Many families are here, and until yesterday all of them strangers. But today we are all connected by someone in the operating room or the intensive care unit.

I would come to know this world very well. We sat there off and on for four months.

*

Our ordeal began on Monday, January 27th, at about six o'clock in the evening. Beth called to ask me to come immediately to take care of her six-year-old son, Jake, so she could take her husband, John, to the emergency room. Something was wrong with his leg.

We decided to meet in the emergency room at a small community hospital in her town. They were taking him from there by ambulance to Beth Israel Hospital, a major teaching hospital in Boston to have an MRI. I asked the doctor what could be wrong.

"Well," she said, "it could be a blood clot in his leg, or bacteria in his skin."

Many hours later, about two in the morning, Beth called from the hospital to tell me that they were taking John into surgery. The infection had spread. Marian, my older daughter, was with her. They did not go home for three days.

At 5:00 a.m. she called again to say that it was a life threatening illness, the flesh eating disease, necrotizing fasciitis. John's chance for survival was slim, five percent I learned later. He was incubated on a respirator and, if he survived, would be in the hospital for months.

The next day, John's parents, Lois and Preston, came from Providence and the five of us, Beth's in-laws, my two daughters, and I waited and waited in the waiting room designated for families of critical care patients.

Finally a doctor came in and we asked if we could see John.

The nurse prepared us, but nothing could really prepare us. John was so swollen, he was unrecognizable. Probably the only reassuring aspect of those first few hours in the hospital was the level of technology and the care, compassion, and concern of the medical staff.

Friends and relatives streamed in all through the day. Every time friends or family came in we could not help ourselves, we cried.

John's illness was one of those random acts of nature that arrive suddenly and without warning. A life-threatening crisis changed the lives of John, Beth, his parents, their siblings, our extended family, and me. That first day we could not possibly imagine that for months we were going to be in the hospital enduring the ups and downs of his illness and the other medical problems that were part of this dreaded disease.

Necrotizing fasciitis is a bacterial infection caused by a Strep A bacteria which usually enters the body through an opening in the skin. In John's case, there was no evidence of a point of entry or how and why he contracted the disease. It is not contagious. During the first twenty-four hours, the disease begins with a pain in some part of the body and a wound is visible. There is an unquenchable thirst and flu-like symptoms. During the next three or four days, there is intense swelling, a purplish rash appears, the blood pressure drops, the body goes into toxic shock, and the individual becomes unconscious.

The key to overcoming this disease is prompt diagnosis and treatment, surgically cutting away the infected areas, and administering large doses of antibiotics. In the United States,. there are approximately 1500 cases per year with a 20% death rate. Survival usually involves removal of infected skin and eventual grafting of new skin. Amputation is often the only remedy if the muscle or bone have been attacked. John was fortunate. The infected areas were all surgically removed before the infection spread to the muscle.

By Wednesday, he was still seriously ill, but now the doctors gave him a 25% chance of survival. Again, he was in surgery, this time to remove more of the infected skin. We were not in the hospital for even forty-eight hours, but felt as if we had been there for at least a month.

We quickly developed a routine. I brought blankets and pillows from home so Beth and Marian would be more comfortable sleeping in the waiting room all night. I picked up Jake after school, gave him dinner, and put him to bed. After taking him to school in the morning, I went to the hospital to be with Beth, Marian, and John's parents. Stephen, my son, came whenever he could. It was a busy time for him, but he made it to the hospital almost daily. Peter, John's closest friend, and his wife Cynthia, seemed to be there all the time, taking turns—they have young children—bringing something to eat, offering any kind of help we would need.

*

For the most part, John's treatment mirrored the usual process for fighting this illness. During the first phase, John was sedated for several weeks, and kept on a ventilator while they tried to stop the spread of the infection. The sedation and ventilator also allowed him to harness all his strength so he did not have to struggle to breathe and endure the continuous pain.

As the body parts began to function normally, the big issue became pain management. The wounds were dressed several times a day, apparently a very painful procedure.

It was especially difficult to watch how helpless John was because he was an athlete. He was a tennis pro. His friends and long-term colleagues visited and told us stories about how he was carving out a new direction in the health and fitness world for people fifty and over.

After the third day, Beth tried to go home every night to give Jake dinner and put him to bed. His one question was, "Will Daddy remember me?"

The support of family and friends sustained us; people seemed to come from unexpected places to help us, bringing food to the hospital, calling people, and just sitting with us for long hours. Even Jake, who was six at the time, is very close to his mother, and does not like other people taking care of him, was cooperative. He would just ask simply, "who is picking me up today?"

*

Throughout John's treatment, the waiting room was a magnet. We knew John wouldn't change in the next few hours, but we stayed. We were afraid to be away. And we were consolation for each other.

Cell phones were ringing all the time. Whose was it? They all sounded the same. Cell phones are a lifesaver in the waiting room. You don't need quarters, people can reach you and you can reach them.

We were the longest-lasting family there. People brought us all kinds of goodies, home-baked cookies, nuts, drinks, fruits, candy. David, John's brother, flew in from Egypt and slept there every night. The hospital nurses provided a cot for him. We sat and sat, and sat, sometimes we visited John, made a phone call, used the rest room. But mainly we sat. We couldn't read, we just sat and were always tired. Why? We did not do anything. But we were always tired.

We came to know David very well, his quiet gentleness, his intelligence, his feelings for his parents, and his commitment to social issues through his work. It took seventeen hours for David to get here from Cairo, and he immediately took on the burden of sleeping in the waiting room overnight, never complaining, helping his parents, keeping watch for all of us during the night.

And Beth cried, thinking about her husband, his long recovery, trying to organize herself, her child, and his care. Although John was unconscious, she went into his room often, kissing him and whispering that everything will be all right. She, too, had a long road ahead. She had to take over John's role at their fitness center.

Resiliency, bonding, and sharing captured the mood of this waiting room culture. We were a family, bonded together with this random illness. There was no need to talk, just being together was bonding.

We probably all had the same fears, but we did not voice them. Will John make it? If he does, will he be incapacitated? How is Beth? How can we help her? This was my daughter, my youngest. I worried all the time about what I could do to ease her burdens, help her share her feelings. We all worried about Jake, their son, only six, how would he fare? Actually, Jake was doing quite well under the circumstances. He was sleeping well, and the school reported that he was fine there.

After the infection in John's body was controlled, skin grafts were taken from his good leg, stretched, and surgically implanted in the infected areas. In some ways, John was fortunate. The infected areas were all surgically removed before the infection had spread to the bone.

By the end of the second week, we knew it was time to go about our daily responsibilities, work, teaching, going to the supermarket. We tried, but we kept going back to the waiting room. Wait for another word from the doctors, wait in case there was a good word about John's condition, wait, in dread, for another crisis. In twos and threes we walked down to the intensive care unit, called on the intercom to see if this was a good time to see John. We would go in, look again at all the technology, read the monitors assuring us his blood pressure was normal, his heart beating as it should. We touched John's arm gently, spoke a few words to him, the nurse said he might be able to hear. Beth would kiss him, tell him she loved him. And we would go back to the waiting room to sit and wait. We had no other place to go, nothing else we wanted to do. Our hearts were there.

John was in the intensive care unit for four weeks. He had six surgeries during that time. He generally proceeded in a slow, but positive direction. John began to have reconstructive surgery, moving two steps ahead and one step back. The first week he had three surgeries, one on Wednesday for eight hours, a call back to surgery at 10:30 that night, and Friday, five hours, for another emergency. Finally, the microsurgery was moving to a positive phase.

During the fourth week, he was moved out of intensive care. The sixth week he was transferred to a rehabilitation center. John went back to the hospital several times for additional surgery, but was slowly progressing to recovery. He was also interviewed on public radio about his illness and his attitude. "I am alive, I enjoy the sunrise, and the sunset, and my glass of orange juice in the morning. To have so much love from family and friends is phenomenal."

And John was right. The family bonding was real for all of us. We learned each other's rhythm and understood how to chime in, when to move back, and when to wait. One moment we were thrilled he was alive, the next despondent about the long convalescence. But he would live.

My Parents, Ida and Nathan Kapilow

John, Beth and Jake

Anne, Stephen Michael, Jonathan, Megan

Marian, Justin, Todd, George

PART 3

Milestones

Our house

What makes a house a home? Is it the physical space, nature that surrounds it...or is it the people who live in that home and the relationships that evolve?

14

The House

It was the day before I would never own the house again. The next day was the closing. I came to broom-sweep the house, to sweep away the dirt and dust left by the movers two days earlier, the dirt that was in corners, under heavy furniture, the dust caught in moldings. We lived in that house for twenty-five years. Perhaps I really came to sweep away my sadness, to sweep away my ambivalence.

Should I have sold? Did I make a terrible mistake? All the furniture was gone; all the concrete reminders of our lives there were gone. Only my memories and images of who we were and what we became remained. I thought about all the people who were part of that house, my parents, my family, my brothers and sister, my former husband, my friends, the women who cared for my children while I studied and worked, my children, the man in my life, and me.

What makes a house a home? What nurtures the soul? Is it the physical space? Is it the surrounding area—the nature, woods, or water views? Or is it the people who lived in that home and the relationships which evolved over years? Is it the activities that took place, the children's birthday parties, the holiday dinners, Thanksgiving, the Passover Seders, eating ice-cream around the dining room table when everyone should be in bed? And what about the material things—my mother's dining room table, my grandmother's candlesticks, the second-hand bureau, and the new lamp that I loved.

"Our house" was an old-style Tudor built in 1929 in Great Neck, a town on Long Island. On the first floor, there were the living and dining rooms, a small bedroom, even smaller den, kitchen, and bathroom. On the second floor, there were three bedrooms and one bath. The basement was for laundry, play, and storage. Only the kitchen had been remodeled.

In my eyes, the house was beautiful even though I knew it was dingy. I never had enough money to fix everything that needed repair or painting. But now the children were grown and gone. What did I need it for? It was time for a change. From what to what, I wasn't sure, but indeed time for a change.

As I looked around that day before the closing, I thought about the past, twenty-five years of living, of loving, of crying, my three children growing up here, leaving home, creating their own lives. This was the place where I grew from dependent wife to emancipated woman, from homemaker to professional, where I became an adult whose sexuality and intelligence finally found release.

What did it mean to sweep these floors, to see the dust and the rust on the floors in the den where my file cabinets stood? Over the course of our long time in that house, the den had three different lives. First it was a room for my ex-husband, the ham radio operator. He put in the black and white tiles on the floor and built the desk. After the divorce, it became my son's room. The hooks for his clothes were still there. For several years he had hamsters in a cage under the window. The noises those hamsters made at night as they went round and round in the cage reverberated through the entire house. So many times I tried to persuade him to get rid of those hamsters! When he was ready, he did.

The third life of this room was my office, the birthplace of my professional life. This pre-computer vintage room held a vast collection of books, papers, work, typewriters, carbons, and paper clips. Those paper clips were always falling no matter how carefully we cleaned. Here I struggled over my dissertation, writing, rewriting, and typing over and over again in the early hours while the children still slept. Today, editing without a computer is difficult to remember or imagine.

This room was also the life of the bills. They were always shuffled, this month, next month, which ones to pay, which could be paid next month. Each day's mail brought new ones. There was no end to the life of the bills.

The funny thing about sweeping the house was that, as usual, I didn't have the right equipment. We never had the right equipment, we never had the right tools, we never had the right lawn mower, but somehow it all stuck together. The broom was too large and the dustpan too small and some of the dirt I swept under the radiators.

Saying Good-bye

On that last day, I also brought my wash. My new apartment did not have a washing machine and a large bundle of dirty laundry had accumulated in just two days. I had a strange feeling as I loaded the washing machine in the basement. How many washes had I done in these machines, from diapers to fancy blouses? How many times did the machines need repair?

Basements are strange and funny places. They are a collection of the potpourri of one's life. Most of the time you could hardly get past the boxes, the old furniture and children's toys. And now the basement was empty, it didn't have anything in it except the washer, dryer, and two boxes of logs for the fireplace.

The basement was large enough for the children to use their bicycles and skates in the winter. That day as I stared at the empty basement I also remembered the dancing lessons we took with other couples when we were married. Each week we would move the toys and bikes out of the way to have room for the six dancing couples. We had so much fun, and yet it turned out to be the kiss of death for a number of couples. At least four or five couples separated or divorced afterward.

The boiler for hot water and heat was also in the basement. I remembered all my worries about the boiler. Is it working? Is there enough heat? Is it making too much noise? The boiler was a key responsibility in my new role as head of the household. It was the old fashioned kind of furnace and on its side was a gauge indicating when the tank needed to be refilled. Too many times I almost forgot that chore until the water line was almost at the bottom. Once I asked a guest to fill the gauge. He forgot to turn the water off and the basement was flooded. We called the plumber, it was an emergency, and I worried that the boiler was ruined forever. I never delegated that job to anyone else again. The cost of replacing the tank was too much to contemplate.

My ex-husband had laid the tiles in the basement, the tiles that my children could ride their bicycles on. That was in the early days of living in that house, the days of promise, of laying new floors, painting the kitchen, and planting shrubs. Over the years from all that activity, the tiles simply wore out and I replaced them to make the house more marketable when I decided to sell.

We had a large freezer in the basement. It was my mother's and she gave it to us when she moved from a house to an apartment.

When it was time for us to move it, to clean the basement for the next family, the movers could not get it up the stairs without removing the banister my husband had built for the children to go up and down the stairs. Along with many other concrete memories of him, that banister was now gone, too.

As you entered our house, you walked into a tiny lobby with closets and then right into the living room. Our living room was always such a wonderful place. Everyone said it was warm and cozy. It wasn't fashionable or chic. It was a room for living, a place where you put your feet on the big red couch, where children, relatives, my friends, their friends all gathered together in front of the fire.

As I stood in the living room that morning, many different images cropped up, particularly memories of their teenage years. There were all these boys, languishing on the couch, waiting for Marian or Beth. Here Stephen and his friend Michael demonstrated their wrestling prowess as Beth and I huddled on top of the sofa, embracing each other for safety, listening to their grunts as they ferociously nailed each other to the floor. They were both on the high school wrestling team.

And the bookshelves in the living room—how I loved the bookshelves! The shelves that I finally put in the living room on the far walls, two walls covered plus the doorway. I could spread my books out, books of all kinds, paperbacks and workbooks, novels, biographies and autobiographies. We had books in every room of the house.

One of the hardest parts about moving was which books to sell and which to keep. I donated several boxes to a library. After moving, I went back to that library and asked for permission to go to the basement and take back as many books as I could find. Even though I would probably never read any of them again and really had no room in a small apartment, I missed my books.

When real estate agents brought in people to see the house, I could hear them talking about having to remodel the kitchen. I never understood what they meant because we thought the kitchen was perfect. Charly, my ex-husband, designed the kitchen and for us, it was absolutely wonderful—all the cabinets, the wood block for chopping, the easy access to the stove and refrigerator. My children learned to cook in that space, barbecue sauce, and spaghetti, and Lindy-like cheesecake. Why would anyone remodel such a splendid kitchen?

My favorite room was the dining room. This room held my mother's dining room table with all the wonders of the Passover feasts, Thanksgiving dinners, and eating ice cream, lots of ice cream. The legacy of feasting and families going from one generation to the next is an image that cannot ever be erased. Now my daughter, Marian, has that table and we feast in her home with her family, her husband, and two sons.

The dining room also held my mother's old, scratched and massive buffet. Why did I cry when the Salvation Army came and took it away? That buffet was a symbol of the life of my family before I was married as well as my life since. The breakfront held the secrets of two generations. In my mother's house it held her linens, lace tablecloths and party napkins, her silverware, her collections of small antiques, and the English coffee cups my father hated.

What did I keep in there? In that buffet were liquor and children's pictures—a whole drawer of children's pictures and children's letters and report cards. My dissertation data took up another whole drawer—the original monographs, graphs, and tables—I threw all that away when I moved.

The windows in the dining room looked right out to the backyard, the place that we barely used. We had a large, two-car garage and only once did I try to park there; the car was new and I scratched it. The garage opening was too small for the latest models, and it was too far from the sidewalk anyhow, too far to shovel the snow in winter. So we used the garage for bicycles, tools, and barbecues. It leaked because the shingles had blown off and never been replaced. The garage was an eyesore and I took it down before I put the house on the market to enhance the sale. Now the yard looked beautiful. It was early spring and the grass was green, but unfamiliar. What was there of us in that backyard now?

While Marian and Steve were in high school, I became aware of a chair occasionally in the driveway under Steve's window. I would ask them about that chair, what was it doing there? They replied that they took it outside to read and put it there as a reminder to take in at night. The explanation seemed reasonable. Many years later, I found out the real reason. It was just under my son's window and when one of their friends did not want to go to school, they would climb on that chair into his room and spend the day. I was the only working mother at that time. Our house was known as the "hooky house."

*

Walking up the stairs, I remembered how we would leave the folded laundry at the foot of the stairs to avoid an extra trip. There was always something on the first step waiting to be carried up. How many times had I climbed those stairs to go to bed, to get dressed, to attend to a child?

On the second floor, my bedroom was the largest. I slept there almost every night for the last twenty-five years. I could hear the squirrels pattering on the roof outside and see the large tree from the bedroom window the first thing in the morning. I thought about the life of that room, the mystery and magic and tears of the nights in that room.

Standing in the bedroom, the image that came cropping up was the period of waiting for the divorce. Charly had moved into the next room and during the tense months preceding the separation, my bedroom was my only sanctuary. Away from the world, alone in the big bed, I felt safe if only for a few minutes.

This bedroom also held memories of love and lovemaking, of newborn Beth sleeping in the crib next to the double bed, of both of us getting up to feed her, enraptured with each other and our new daughter. This was the place where children, waking up in the middle of the night with a bad dream, would snuggle in for comfort. It was in this room, in the middle of those long, sleepless nights, that I realized I had to rebuild my life and take care of my children.

The second bedroom, the one next to mine, had its own history. How many lives have lived in that room? Marian and Stephen slept there, then Marian and Beth slept there, then Marian slept there, then Beth and her dog, Ralph, slept there. Then Gloria slept there, my friend who lived with me for a year after all the children had gone. In two large bookcases, Richard, my former lover, stored a lifetime of his love of books when he came to live with me the last year I owned the house.

Those last moments, walking through the house, I wept for all that had been and all that might have been, for the dreams one has and the fantasies about what life could be. And then for all the surprises, for some of them were very good.

Final Moments

Many years later after I sold the house, during the year I lived and worked in Israel, I went to dinner with a colleague, his wife, and teenage daughter. We were celebrating the publication of his new book. A young couple in their thirties came by to congratulate my colleague. "When we get home to Great Neck," she said, "we will tell everyone about your book."

"Who are you?" I asked. "I come from Great Neck."

And they told me. I gasped, they were the people who bought my house. I understood why I didn't recognize them and started to cry. Leaving that house and what it symbolized was so difficult for me. Does the pain never leave?

This was the couple who wanted to meet me before they purchased the house and wanted to know about my life there. I told them, "This house has a soul."

I loved that house. I knew its creaks; I knew the sound of the boiler. I could tell when the washing machine wasn't working just by the sound. I remember the bell, its strong resonant persistence, and the reassurance of the radiator noises on those long, cold nights. A house is like a person. Over time, you learn its strengths, its vulnerabilities, where to go easy, where to press hard. You know what to fix, what to leave alone, what not to impose on, what to use to its fullest.

In that house, there was so much unfinished business, unresolved feelings, former angers, uncut lawn, a dilapidated garage. I always feared that I had left something on when I went out, like the coffee pot, or the electric blanket. Or maybe the furnace wasn't working correctly. There was always so much to do, so much to fix, to accomplish, to resolve with the children. Bills needed to be paid, articles had to be written, old lovers buried, and childhood fears extinguished.

The house symbolized the divorce, the various life styles, the friendships, the women, the men, the values, the breaking up, and the growing up. It also represented the fears, the exhilaration, the weeping, the laughter, and the insomnia. How many nights I had insomnia in that house! The house was my past, my growing up, my children growing up. It was the metaphor for family, for love, for identity, the place where I began and fulfilled a career. It was the place where my identity as a woman, as a mother, as an educator, as a human being was formed.

The house also symbolized the unity in our lives. It helped us struggle with the rootlessness of divorce, helped us feel anchored, helped me feel sheltered. Whenever my children came home, almost twenty years later, they still drove past "our house" to see what is the same, what is different, to show their own children where they were born and where they grew up.

Most of the time we lived in that house, the side door was open, open for service people and for us, we hated to be bothered with keys. That open door symbolized the safety and openness we felt there. The doors were open to our possibilities as individuals and as a family.

Does our love of the house represent the lost dream, the dream of marriage and living happily ever after, the tight-knit family? Was the dream real or illusory? Does one long forever for what might have been? The irony is that the dream stifled my becoming, the smashing of the dream brought confidence. And neither the dream nor the shelter of the house protected me from pain, loneliness, or feelings of betrayal.

We loved the house, and the house loved us. Look what the house gave us. I never wrote one single poem before I sold that house, before I stood in that kitchen, in that living room, and those bedrooms and thought about the meaning of the house, the love of the house, the vitality of that house. It gave each of us a connection, a connection to it and to each other.

That house gave us its strengths, its imperfections, its cracks, and its warmth. It let us grow up and not be pretentious, helped us learn both simplicity and complexity. The house loved us so much it gave us the strength, the wisdom, and the time to live on and on no longer in it.

This story ends with a recent summer, thirty-two years after I sold the house. I was going back to Great Neck to visit an old friend and had a strong desire to see my house once more. I needed to say goodbye again. I called Abby, she remembered me, and I asked if I could come and visit. "Of course," she said, "come on over." She greeted me with, "you were right, this house has a soul."

15

The Empty Nest: A Second Time Around

My grandchildren are growing up and moving on to lives of their own. Their departure has left me feeling sad and lonely. It's an empty nest syndrome that I didn't feel when my own children left.

Marian and Steve are eighteen months apart and Beth is five years younger. Gradually, they went to college and forged career plans. But my home was their home and they would come there for weekends, holidays, and summers. We had a pact, each one would call at least once a week.

I was still working, absorbed and passionate about my career, which took the edge off those empty nest feelings. Different people lived with me over the years, a friend who separated from her husband, another friend who relocated from California, and Richard, my on-again, off-again lover. I was free now to go to India, Cyprus, and Israel without worrying about the children. One by one they graduated from college, enrolled in graduate programs, found interesting work, married, and had children of their own.

They moved to Boston for different reasons. Marian's soon-to-be-husband, George, lived and worked there and after getting her degree in Pennsylvania she moved to Boston. Steve met Anne in college, she was from Boston, and after he acquired his law degree landed a great job in Boston. Beth worked in New York after graduating from college but after ten years said, "I am leaving this city because I am tired of putting on my lights in the middle of the day." She decided to live near her siblings, moved to Boston, and met her husband, John, there.

They married, had their own children, and now I had this family of twelve people, six adults and six children all living in Boston. My children and their spouses turned out to be great parents and all the grandchildren have the right values, interesting careers, and independence.

I came to Boston about once a month. Driving seemed a snap while listening to books on tape. Some people worried, "You drive all by yourself back and forth to Boston?" I did not understand what the problem was.

Marian, Steve, and Beth would come down with their families for the holidays or school vacations and stay for periods of days. Before Beth married, there could be ten of us in my two bedroom apartment. The children slept in sleeping bags on the floor. As my grandmother used to say, "If there is room in your heart, there is room in your home." We were together, enjoying our growing family and it was fun being in close quarters, enjoying the grandchildren as they played with their cousins

I also owned a house in East Hampton, the equivalent of the Cape in Massachusetts but, according to this former New Yorker, much better. At least, the water isn't freezing and you could actually swim in the ocean. My family would come, taking three ferries from New London to Orient Point, to Shelter Island, and then to Sag Harbor.

They came for days at a time and I was so happy when the adults would go out to dinner and I could stay with the grandchildren. It was a ritual for my son, his wife, and their three children to spend every spring vacation in the Hamptons. I have a book of photographs for each year catching the children building sand castles on windy dunes and climbing the cliffs in Montauk. Often on my trips to Boston I baby-sat. Though I still lived in New York, I always felt part of their lives.

By the time I retired, my most recent personal relationship was over, and most of my friends were moving. I decided to take the big plunge and relocate to Boston. I could be comfortable there. In addition to family, I had, off and on through the years, various professional roles in the Harvard educational community and knew some people.

I found a great apartment, and, with the help of the people I knew and then met, and my family, quickly felt at home. Here in Boston, I was part of their lives but in a different way. I went to soccer and hockey games, saw the grandchildren in school plays, went to grandparents' day, and baby-sat. It was not the experience that came with their visits to New York for several days, but here in Boston I was part of their day-to-day lives on a regular basis.

But children grow up, and grandchildren grow up, too. And one by one they left for college and graduate schools. Now some are working but in different cities, not Boston. Who knows, they may be all over the map in a few years.

It is the empty nest all over again but different from the first time around. I do not get the weekly calls—I don't know if their parents do either. They probably use the computer or Facebook to communicate. If and when they come home, it is to their parents' home. Sometimes I feel lucky if I can see them at least for an hour or two.

This second time around is not as easy, at least for me.

16

About Men: The Recurrent Dilemma

In a fashionable two-block radius in Great Neck, the town where I lived, an area of elegant apartment houses, trees, and expensive cars, lived the three men who sequentially inhabited approximately thirty-five years of my life. There was Charles, my husband for seventeen years, my first lover, Richard, for twelve years, and finally, Sidney, for seven. Two of them lived in the same building. They did not know each other. But they mirrored each other in so many ways, where they lived, what they were about as human beings, how they felt about women. They were all bright, accomplished achievers, and I had great times with each of them. But we could never transcend the difficulties.

I was married at twenty, right after graduation from college; Charly was beginning on the G.I. Bill of Rights. Why did I marry him? What did I know? I knew he loved me, admired me, and thought me pretty and smart. He was a great dancer. I could talk to him, and he would listen, no matter what I had to say about anything. I wasn't sure when I married him whether or not I really loved him, I was too young to know. How does one know for sure? I had been socialized to view marriage as the most important goal in a woman's life. I was led to believe that the route to happiness—the only route—was to become wife and mother. At that time of my life, the thought of combining marriage with a career never entered my mind.

My mother had two things to say about dating, marriage, and sex. When I was a teenager, she told me to "never let a boy know how smart you are." The night before I married, she warned me, "always take a shower before you are intimate with your husband."

Sadly, my mother believed that females were second-class citizens, subservient to their husbands, who had the power. And sex was a chore. I didn't believe my mother had anything valid to say, but what else could I do after I graduated from college? I had no career aspirations at that time, but I knew it was time to leave my parents' home.

Charly was gentle and quiet, so different from my intense, gregarious, difficult father. We had many good years together—when the children were born and young were the best. I grew to really love him. He could cook, fix anything, and knew how to take care of the children, diaper and feed them as well as I did. We had lots of friends, played bridge, went to dinner parties, and made love. We took pleasure in each other's achievements, took dancing lessons with five other couples in our basement, and were generally satisfied with our lives. Our greatest pleasure together was watching our children grow and blossom.

Although I believe in "till death do us part," love can die and new attachments can form. What is most difficult to accept and understand is how a person who was once my spouse, the father of our children, the one who slept next to me for so many years, could turn so quickly into an adversary. What was the process that changed him, his view of the world, and what he wanted? He became besotted with money, wanting more all the time. His work was going well, and our children were growing in ways we applauded. We lived in an affluent community, and he had a great position with the school system. But what changed him in relation to me? The level of his cruelty during the entire year of the ongoing divorce proceeding was unbelievable. Where did that cruelty come from? And why?

The prospect of divorce was hard enough but the realities were almost unbearable. Divorce is like a jungle filled with fear of the unknown, sudden and unexpected dangers, predatory animals, issues of survival, and the treatment of lawyers and judges, all male, with their smart suits, briefcases, and indifference to your fears and concerns about money. We worked out a plan including visitation with the children. Only once did he take them overnight, but he did see them every Wednesday and Sunday and the children felt close to him.

But why did he sell my car? We lived in suburbia, there was no way to get around without a car, and I was part of a cooperative nursery school and car-pooled. Why did he come into the house when I wasn't home, take the one television set we had and the nails from the basement? He seemed crazy. It was not only me he was punishing, it was his children. Why did he lack any generosity for his children's financial and medical needs?

It turned out that he was having an affair with one of my friends. I found out months later, shortly before they were married. He started our marriage with "I love you," and ended it with, "send them clean." He was getting married, and wanted the children clean and well-dressed for his wedding.

After Charly's second divorce and a long battle with illness, he lived with my older daughter. When I visited we were always cordial, going out to lunch, enjoying the grandchildren, preparing together for the wedding of our younger daughter. There were occasional glimpses of his early gentleness, of those values I respected. But he resisted any possibility of talking about what happened. I don't know why. My anger had diminished long ago. He remained a mystery to me forever.

*

Men have never been my strongest suit. Sure, there have been enough of them. After Charly I had a propensity for men who were remote, hard to get, exciting for a moment, and then away they went. Was this a legacy from my mother and her warnings and wonderful "advice?" I never could figure it out.

I met Richard three years after my divorce. He was not a prince, but a prince charming; he came back and forth into my life, exuding charm, fun, and passion. As soon as we had real intimacy, he would flee again. Each time he came back, he said this is the last time, and I always believed him. We were together, off and on, for twelve years.

It was so hard to give up the promise. Richard shared my love for the outdoors. We were both so proud and busy getting our doctorates. We traveled, went skiing, visited art museums, and began white-water rafting and canoeing. Films were a passion for both of us and I still remember going to the movies with Richard, sitting close to him, holding hands, and talking later about what it all meant.

Some of the greatest beaches in the world are on Long Island. For hours we would sit side by side, reading or sleeping, then ride the waves and eat lunch. We loved the sun, the sand, the water, and each other.

We both loved ice cream and I remember the second date in Tanglewood, laughing as we sat at the counter ordering flavor after flavor. We ate tons of ice cream on vacations, even in the middle of the night. Together we would decide which flavor to buy, his favorite or mine, often, some of each.

We shared the same values about children, money, and friends. I remember the fun Richard and my children had trying to duplicate Lindy's cheesecake. For a long time I missed Richard bringing good fruit to the house, listening to him talk about what was going on in the world, and what was happening to the Jewish people..

Often it was idyllic. But there are just so many times you can fall in and out of love with the same person. The game Richard played diminished both of us. When I became strong, it ended.

But I still miss him.

*

Since my divorce, men have been part of my consciousness, despair, joys, and life style. In one way or another, I had to find out how to meet men in the single culture of our times, how to keep them, and how to let them go. I don't know which is harder, finding them or letting them go.

By the time of the divorce, my feelings for Charly had dissipated so it wasn't hard letting go. Although I loved Richard, there were so many beginnings and endings as dress rehearsals for the final one. Sidney was the hardest one to let go. I don't know why, really. Maybe because I was older, more open to compromise. Maybe what kept me tied to him was the apprehension that he might be the last man in my life. He wasn't.

Sidney was the most powerful man I have known. He was a successful businessman, and I was impressed by his authority. He was tall, broad, and very handsome. He knew all the best restaurants, loved to wander through New York, was a fast driver, and never let his defenses down. When my younger daughter graduated from college and needed an apartment in New York, he found one for her.

Sidney was a scuba diver. We went all over the world traveling to new places for him to scuba dive. I am a fairly good swimmer, gutsy in a way, but would never have dreamed of starting scuba diving without Sidney. Some days, we would swim out to the middle of the bay off some lovely Caribbean Island with our snorkels and masks, and explore the world underwater. We walked along the beach, climbed the rocks, roamed endlessly. I felt adventurous, yet safe and secure with Sidney as my guide.

But Sidney wanted it all free. He wanted to have me in his life, have fun when he wanted, and not take any responsibility for anything more. He needed total control to do it his way, call all the shots. What was powerful and productive in his work was finally not reasonable in a relationship. I had been through too much to settle, and we drifted apart.

I mourned the loss for a long time. Endings are often beginnings, but it was hard to leave without looking back, wondering would anything have changed if I faced life differently. For awhile, I felt as if I were sleep-walking through life and convalescing from a major illness. Eventually, my life force came back. I couldn't mourn forever. It was time to get on with my life.

I often wonder about these three men, Charly, Richard, Sidney. I knew them for such a long period of my life. They lived within walking distance of each other and me, but sometimes it seemed as if they lived on the other side of the world. At the same time, there were many wonderful and meaningful times with each of them.

The most difficult part was finding my own reality, transcending the culture and what I had been brought up to believe. I grew up in a couple's culture. I did finally find myself in terms of my intelligence and competence and am proud of those qualities. Despite the difficulties, I relished the liberation of being a single parent. I do know now that everyone has to reconcile the limitations of one's life, with some early goal that is never reached. Not everything can be achieved. Perhaps meeting the right person, someone I could be comfortable with, someone who understands reciprocity and mutuality rather than power, is not in the cards for me. We seem not to attract each other and I find peace in the acceptance and understanding.

The journey of life does not go forward in a single straight line; there are unexpected curves and reverses. I had choices. But I still wonder, am I a failure without a special man in my life? Am I a success because I know what I want and need and cannot endure less? I only know the answers to these questions for fleeting moments. Much of the time, the truth eludes me.

17

Mirror, Mirror on the Wall

When I moved to Boston n the late nineties, I bought one of those skinny wall mirrors. As soon as I looked into it in the store, I realized this particular mirror made me look thin, or at least thinner. The reflection reminded me of my old self. Now, whenever I get dressed to go out, the last thing I do is look in this mirror. This last glance, whether real or fantasy, reminds me of my younger days and provides some sort of reassurance.

Once when my sister came to visit she looked into that mirror and said how thin it made her look. Before my next visit to her, I went back to that hardware store to buy another "skinny" mirror. I lined up about five mirrors and asked the salesclerks to help me figure out which made them look the skinniest. They could not stop laughing. I put the chosen mirror in the car, and when I reached New York, dragged it through the streets from my parking place to her apartment. She was thrilled.

This thin mirror is always reassurance because no matter how many miles I run or how many diets I follow, I always feel fat. If I eat one cookie, I feel as if my stomach is bulging. Why do I always think fat no matter how thin I am or how many size eights I buy? No matter how many people tell me "How thin you are," why do I always feel fat? Even though my clothes hang and are loose, I think fat, I feel fat. Is it the corsets of my youth, the weight-reducing machines, or my mother's obsession? Is it the crazy world we live in where the most beautiful people in the world pictured in the style section of Sunday's *New York Times* are always svelte?

The battle of the bulge is a burden that is not eliminated with running, dieting, and people's compliments, but the skinny mirror helps. My mother was obsessed about being thin, particularly for her daughters. It had something to do with being able to get married. My sister was always on the heavy side, a problem that plagued her all her life. One day my parents discovered that she stole my brother's bottles from his crib. For weeks my mother wondered why my brother was always crying. She believed that stealing the bottle was an early indication of Milly's appetite. I am convinced her weight had very little to do with her eating habits. I believe she had a different metabolic system.

My mother enrolled us in a weight-reducing place called MacLevy's. I don't think it exists today. My role was to keep my sister company. MacLevy's consisted of a variety of machines for losing weight. If we sat on one for twenty minutes twice a week, the fat would just roll off. If only it were that easy.

Usually, my father picked us up when we were finished with our machine routines. He had such a need to subvert everything my mother believed in that he took us out for malteds or spaghetti on the way home. It was a secret, and we were not to tell our mother. Whether it was the crazy machines or the malteds or spaghetti, neither my sister nor I ever lost a pound or inch during that time.

My mother's worries proved true. My sister never did marry. It was not for the lack of men in her life, there were several. Nor did it have anything to do with size. For whatever reason, it was her choice.

Conversations about weight and health—thin, fat, obese—have taken over America. Several years ago, a famous opera star was denied the right to sing because the director said she was too heavy. Opera is a world where size was never a factor, look at Pavarotti. The specific part called for her to wear a "little black dress" which, of course, was not possible. The director was not concerned about her health but whether she looked the part. She finally went on a diet.

Although I hate to admit it, I do understand the director. The obsession for me is not about health, it is about aesthetics.

I once heard Carol Gilligan, a well-known research psychologist, speak. Her main interest is women's development. She interviewed women across the country from all walks of life and social classes and the one thing they all seemed to revere was "being thin." Several years ago, Debora Spar, President of Barnard College talked about modern feminism at the Harvard Business School. "Women in positions of power," she said, "are expected to be thin, attractive, and in shape."

As an adult, I was the thinnest after my divorce. Although the divorce process and its aftermath were a nightmare, there was something reassuring about looking into the mirror and seeing my size six body. I lost my appetite and my weight dropped very quickly. When I see someone now, male, or female, someone I've known for a long time, and they seem much thinner, it usually is a divorce. I can spot the "divorce thin look" a mile away. And I am 99% right.

I think the best years of my life, physically speaking, were the years between forty and sixty. Divorced and liberated, I was very conscious of my looks. I had no one to please but myself and could wear the kind of clothes I liked. I began to dress more stylishly. I traveled, I was a professional, I worked abroad. I was a woman of the world, wasn't I? I had to look the part.

When I look into any mirror now, I am usually surprised. The reflection is not what I expect to see. I am not the young girl of my twenties, the lovely young mother in my thirties rearing a family, the sophisticated divorced, professional woman of my forties and fifties. I am definitely older; there are lines and creases. How did they get there and when? Often I see my mother's face. The glimpse startles me. We are mirrors of each other. Wrinkles and weight, I am uneasy with the brush of time. Where is my skinny mirror?

18

I Want

I want to eat all the chocolate ice-cream
I want without getting fat.

I want to find an apartment in New York
that I can afford, with a terrace and wonderful
view of the harbor.

I want never to go into therapy again.

I want to be surrounded by
gifted people who
think grand thoughts,
are never petty, and love me
no matter what I do.

I want to know I'll
never have cancer or become
a cabbage in my old age, that I'll always
be financially independent.

I want my ex-husband
to approve of me,
tell me how much he thinks I've accomplished

since the divorce, and what a good job I did
bringing up the children.

I want to get a really good night's sleep.

I want to be one of those people who is always
coming back from some exotic place
having a grand adventure
traveling alone on a shoestring.

I want to ride my bike
down long, narrow,
country trails again.

I want to live a conventional life
but have everyone think I'm adventurous
offbeat and exciting.

I want to have a lover who's good in bed
I want to be proud of him. I want him not to be
into games or power. I want him to
love me and be committed to me,
and I want to do my own thing and
not be bothered too much.

I want all women to be successful
and smart and believe in the
right causes, and be wonderful.
I want to be proud of them. I want
that for men too, but not as much.

I don't want everybody to like me
because that means I don't stand
for anything, but I want the right
people to like me.

I want to be able to take a few drags
on a cigarette occasionally without
becoming a smoker again.

I want to write a really good poem.

PART 4

Challenge and Choice

The divorce, once so traumatic, liberated me to find a totally new journey....

19

Finding My Own Road–The Working Life

For a very long time, I never considered a career or a direction. Ambition was not on my mind.

During college, I worked the typical New York jobs that young, middle-class women had during the holidays and summers—salesgirl at department stores such as Bloomingdales and Macys or the glamorous but now defunct Wannamaker. One year, I sold stockings at Miles Shoe store on 125th Street in Harlem, finishing on Christmas Eve and walking down 125th Street close to midnight to take the subway home.

In the summer I worked as a camp counselor, once at Lake Mohegan in a community where my parents had a summer home and another time at a sleep-away camp owned by a friend's parents. I am a very good swimmer and one year had a job as the lifeguard in our community lakefront. On that job, I vacillated between periods of extreme boredom to fear of what to do if someone was in trouble in the water.

Immediately after graduation, I married and our goal was for me to work Charly's way through college and graduate school. He was a veteran going to school on the G.I. Bill of Rights.

For a few years, I had a series of low-level jobs, secretary, bookkeeper, personnel assistant. One of them, for the Unemployment Insurance Office, even required a college degree. But that job as "interviewer" consisted basically of asking people little more than, "did you work last week?"

I soon realized that I could not bear the thought of working at those jobs for four or five years. Since Charly was planning on graduate school, we decided that I should get a graduate degree too. My life would be more satisfying, and there would be more income after the year of sacrifice.

I considered social work, my college major. But it took two years to become a social worker, and we could not afford two years of study for me. Finally, I matriculated for a one-year master's degree in education. I thought of it simply as a credential to help support the coming years of his study. Yet the year turned out to be a surprising and inspiring experience. Some of the giants in teacher education at the time were on the faculty at Teachers College, Columbia University. It was the first time I fully grasped the excitement of being in an intellectual community and glimpsed my own competence. Sometimes we could only afford tomato sandwiches for dinner, but it didn't matter because I was so excited by what I was doing.

I became a teacher, taught for several years at the elementary level, and kept the marriage afloat financially. Friends advised me to make sure I gave my salary check to my husband so that I would not detract from his masculinity. I never disputed the idea, it was intrinsic to our culture.

After the children were born, I gave up full-time work, but kept my hand in the workplace through substituting, working in the summers, teaching English as a second language, and religious school. The goal was simply to increase our income. At the same time, I was teaching in various settings and began to grasp and understand the complexities of education in our country and who was served and who wasn't.

Slowly, over time, I began to feel the restlessness and confinement of not searching for a career. I repressed those feelings, however, never considering the possibility of combining a career with mothering and marriage. And then the great trauma of my life, the divorce, forced me to rethink who I was and what I needed to do about working.

I had to work because alimony and child support were not enough to sustain us. But doing what? I was afraid to become a teacher on a full-time basis and go back to the classroom. My children were young, what would I do if one was ill or some emergency arose? Higher education seemed to offer more flexibility. With my teaching background I believed I could supervise student teachers during their school placement semester. I sent letters of inquiry to about six universities and colleges with teacher education programs on Long Island.

One of those letters was on a dean's desk at the State University of New York in New Paltz, the morning a member of that faculty slipped on the ice and broke her hip. My exploration paid off. I was offered a temporary position supervising student teachers, to replace the person who was injured. Eventually, I became a permanent member of that faculty.

This was a turning point. In my early years of working, I didn't contemplate the idea of choice, of making decisions about a career; I didn't realize it was appropriate for me to be ambitious. My work evolved with no clear sense of the options regarding my decisions, except, perhaps, practicality. I needed to provide income.

A male psychiatrist I was in treatment with convinced me for two years that I didn't want a doctorate, that what I really wanted was to get married. It never dawned on me that it was possible to do both. Perhaps I procrastinated and followed the psychiatrist's subtle cues because I was afraid of the commitment and concerned about my ability. At the same time, I was in an intellectual setting working with intelligent people each of whom had a doctorate. Finally, my ambition overcame my lack of confidence. I decided, despite the psychiatrist, to get a doctorate, the union card for higher education

The years of study toward the doctorate were exciting and productive. I loved the exhilaration of the intellectual world, the challenge, and the work.

I was again at Columbia, where I earned my master's degree. This time, I was asked to become a working member of a research grant on teacher education sponsored by the Office of Education in Washington. Tuition was now free. In my second year, I became the co-director of the graduate program in teacher education. My dissertation, the first in that program, documented the research and application of the theoretical model.

I lived in the world of high expectations, commuting to New York every day, holding a full-time job, studying in the wee hours of the night, and getting up at five in the morning to write my dissertation before the children needed breakfast. I learned to juggle my various roles and embrace whatever I was doing at the moment—mother, student, teacher, and professional. I began to understand my intellectual and creative abilities and was ecstatic.

This was a new world, a world in which people acknowledged my competence and saw my potential, writing the first dissertation in this new field, getting grants, traveling, doing workshops. My horizons were expanded, personally and professionally. I had a renewed sense of my worth, energy, and creative capabilities.

Just as I was completing the doctorate, I read an article in the *New York Times* about a new experimental college. I wrote a letter, had several interviews and became one of the first faculty members. This experience turned out to be a rare opportunity. We were pioneering a new movement in higher education and the work was challenging and rewarding on every level. From its inception, Empire State College has been on the cutting edge of new programs in higher education for adults and I played a major role in those efforts both within and outside the college.

Empire State College, a unit of the State University of New York, opened its doors in 1972 and consisted of seven learning centers in the State. Now, there are over forty plus several abroad. The design was individualized learning with faculty as mentors and the average age of the students, thirty-six. Many of them had thriving careers, others were seeking a new beginning. The diversity was exciting. A small sample of our student population included police from New York whose schedules changed all the time, people seeking new work lives or credentials, artists, and women who were just beginning a career outside the home.

It was exciting to work with students who were outside the traditional model of higher education. One female student was raped when she was sixteen and, as a result, decided to study Tai Chi. She became an international champion but it was a challenge to convince her that she could also experience success in the academic world. She eventually acquired a doctorate and worked at the highest level of fundraising for several well-known institutions in New York. Another, a welder, became an educator. Many of my former students gained high positions in local government and laboratories on Long Island. The list is long and creates a vision of the possibility for creating exciting possibilities for a new population in higher education.

I was on important committees and developmental projects, conducted research, obtained several grants, and worked with various colleagues disseminating our model to other institutions across the country. In the early days of the college, I was awarded the certificate of excellence, a prestigious award from the State University of New York for one person in each college.

My restless spirit took a new direction as the college administration began exploring models of inter-institutional collaboration abroad, which began my love affair with international education. By then, my children were grown and no longer needed me at home. I had a Fulbright to India and administered a unit in Israel for one year. Cyprus had a different model and I was there five times as a consultant. Another year, I was the administrator of a program based at Stony Brook University on Long Island. I blossomed with each new experience.

What had started out as expedient, a credential to help out in the early days of my marriage, evolved into a major, satisfying career in which I could put into practice all the creative and intellectual abilities which had been dormant for so long.

The divorce, once so traumatic, liberated me to find a totally new journey for myself in the world of work. I discovered personal resources I never knew I had—curiosity, perseverance, competence, stamina, and the ability to pursue excellence. Finally, I learned to take charge of my life, to search and explore what I wanted and needed.

20

The Dawning of Liberation

One summer, at a party in Geneva, Switzerland, I met Marcello. Marcello was from Italy. He was tall, but not too tall, just tall enough for him to look dashing and me to feel comfortable. In the chic style of Europe, he wore a beautiful silk, paisley ascot, contrasting vividly with his white suit, and in turn, the white suit contrasting dramatically with his dark tan.

I was there to experience Europe. My cousin was a vice-president with a large international company based in Switzerland. I asked him if he could get me a job for the summer, any job, so I could explore the continent. And he did. I sent my children to camp and headed to Switzerland for a four-day-a-week position as an administrative assistant. Those long weekends gave me all the opportunities I needed to see Europe.

Marcello represented all the beautiful people I met, people from around the world, sophisticated people with names in newspapers and gossip columns. I went to parties and travelled to Paris and Italy.

"I am the adventurous spirit, the emancipated woman," I wrote home to my family, my mother, and my friends.

Marcello was at a conference in Geneva for a few days and invited me to dinner. I was flattered.

The restaurant he took me to was on a beautiful curve on Lake Luzerne, with candles shimmering on the tables and the moon reflecting on the water. Our table was covered with a pink table cloth topped with a small vase of flowers. Marcello had reserved the quiet, corner table.

I was feeling slightly adolescent in this sophisticated, dramatic setting, and would have preferred Marcello to sit across the table, but he firmly and quietly took the seat next to me. Immediately, his leg pressed gently against mine. I tried to move away, create distance between us, and catch my breath. Slowly sipping the wine he ordered, I felt his hand across my shoulders, slowly moving down my back, mysteriously his leg once again pressing against mine. How did he manage to get so close?

I tried to seem assured, at ease, engaged in conversation while distracting his hands, his roving hands, soothing, and gentle, always somewhere on my body. He was so charming, the question silent on his lips, he was so smart with women and his every move part of the seduction.

Until the divorce, I had never been with any man other than my husband. Now, if I wished, sex was open, there for the tasting, the asking, and the experimenting. Who was I in this new world? One part of me was the emancipated woman, the woman of our time, the intellectual. The other half, monogamous, loyal, fiercely attached to the values of my childhood. I could be persuaded either way.

"Come, let's dance," Marcello said.

"Kiss me once and kiss me twice and kiss me once again," a song from my younger days and memories of other kisses long ago.

Surrendering to his arms, gliding slowly to his touch, his grace, moving together with the music, the strong hand on my back. Did he need to press so hard to lead me to the next step?

The glasses were always full. Slightly flushed with wine, he moved towards me, pressed my knee, talked freely about his life, his travels, his love of women. He asked me gently about my life, "you are a woman of the world," he said, "free, adventurous, not like all the American woman who come to Europe."

Flattering always with the small caress, the sweet politeness, charm, and grace, the anticipation of the long night radiated from his pores, his skin, and his smiling eyes. The evening flowed and I flowed with it—one moment loose, drawn in, connected, the next outside, looking at myself, at him, wondering who am I, what do I want.

On the long walk home, we talked of many things, wine, good food, the music in our heads, his arm around my shoulders, then my waist, moving slowing, gently caressing my back. He told me many things about his education, about Geneva, about Milan, his home, and his favorite Italian author.

"This building is where one hundred Jews were saved," he said, knowing I am Jewish.

We walked and talked, making jokes. I felt free, lighthearted, a woman of the world. Then the old pulls as I slowly backed away.

At my hotel, he gently kissed me, "We will go up. Yes?" he said, "We must, we are simpatico, together, a moment in time, we pass like ships in the night. You a woman from America, me a man from Milan, both free. We are people of the world, enjoy the night," he whispered, his skin, his smiling eyes, alive with promise, "Yes, we will go up."

I looked at him, thought, and knew the answer. For a moment, everything seemed sure, together.

"Freedom," I softly said, "means saying no as well as yes."

21

In Jerusalem

From July 1987 to July 1988, I lived and worked in Israel. I left for Israel two days after my mother died; she had been ill for a long time. Here, in Israel, I grieved for her, discovered new sides of myself, made new connections, and possibly even, found a measure of peace

I was there as temporary director of Empire State College's program in Israel. The children had long since grown, and I was always looking for new opportunities.

When I arrived, slightly nervous but excited, I was immediately entranced. In a taxi from the airport, the seven hills surrounding Jerusalem were beautiful and, to me, a magnetic welcome.

Two weeks after I arrived, I found an apartment in a lovely section of Jerusalem. This was the nicest apartment I ever lived in—comparable to the large, magnificent apartments on the west side of New York City, which I never could afford.

The work was demanding, but immediately satisfying. I tested my philosophy of management and was gratified to be able to put into practice ideas that I had felt strongly about for a long time, principles about supervision and leadership style. Faculty and staff accepted me very quickly and were delighted with my open style of management.

Being away from family, my old work life, the world I knew, and the troubles with which I had become so familiar provided the time and space to reflect on my life and put some difficulties to rest.

Jerusalem is an extraordinary city, including worship settings for Muslims, Jews, and Christians in the Old City.

Shabbat, the Sabbath, is the highlight of the week for the Jewish population in Jerusalem. For most observant Jews the preparation starts on Friday morning. The religious observance begins Friday at sunset and ends Saturday at sunset. People are different on Fridays, hurrying more in the morning as there is so much to do to prepare.

By Friday afternoon, something is in the air, something imperceptible at first. "Shabbat Shalom," a peaceful Sabbath is everywhere—in the grocery, in the streets, in the flower shop. Friends, strangers on the street, and children who echo their parents, say goodbye with the words "Shabbat Shalom," a peaceful Sabbath. In the playground friends and strangers leave each other with the same words, "Shabbat Shalom."

My first Sabbath in Jerusalem I sensed the mood of the city—its tranquility and peaceful atmosphere embraced us all. And now, I was one of its inhabitants and quickly adapted to this feeling of harmony, at least on Shabbat and the Jewish holidays.

My third week in Israel, I was alone for the weekend and decided to go on an organized walking tour of the religious quarter, Meah Shearim, on Friday morning. There were no television antennas in this part of town. All the men and boys wore black suits with white shirts. Girls and women dressed in long sleeves and stockings despite the heat—the women with their heads covered. To me they were people from another time, another century.

A store in which yarmulkes, small religious skullcaps, were made and altered was crowded. "Today is Shabbat, a good day to buy a new one," the tour guide explained.

That night, I went to the Old City to visit the Western Wall. On the bus I met someone who had been on the tour in the morning, John from San Francisco, and we decided to go together.

We arrived early, sat, and watched, mesmerized by the scene. The sun was shining like gold over the stones of the Wailing Wall. As sunset approached, the people began to gather, people from all over the world, another melting pot. Arabs, too, were there; women covered from head to toe walked with their children as they came from the Muslim quarter. At the Wailing Wall, groups of American teenagers danced.

Americans, non-Jews, tourists from around the world, all sat transfixed by the scene. It was impossible not to be caught up in the magic of the moment. John shared his reactions to the sights and sounds we saw and heard together, and wondered about the history and ritual. He was not Jewish and had been invited to Israel to consult with the Histadrut about labor unions, his specialty.

He had never seen Jewish religious rituals and wanted to know more about them. The rituals we witnessed were from ancient times, I explained. They had not changed in a thousand years. Seeing it from the point of view of this stranger who knew nothing about Jewish customs gave me an added appreciation of the history and meaning of the Jewish experience and its impact on modern Israel.

We left to have a bite. It had to be at an Arab restaurant, since all Jewish ones were closed for the Sabbath. After dinner, we said goodnight. As I walked home alone, I heard men singing from an open window near my apartment. I knew those songs. They were ones my grandfather sang every Shabbat back home. It made me feel connected to my own world and to my life experience as an American Jew.

Through the window I saw candles burning brightly on the table as the men sang. The room looked warm and cozy. I walked by, peered in, turned around, and did it again. The warmth of the room radiated, pulled me back again and again.

And then I noticed something that reminded me of how I felt growing up in America and getting married. There was a woman standing beside the table, waiting. Where were the others, the wives of the other men? I had once been alone like that just watching and waiting. And here, again, like her, I was alone and outside.

The next morning, the Sabbath, I awoke with a feeling of personal peace that matched the peace outside. No sounds came from my window of people going to work, no garbage trucks, and no cars. Families walked together, men holding their velvet bags for the synagogue service.

I visited an art exhibition. Like all museums, it was open on the Sabbath and free so that people would not have to handle money. The quiet of the museum echoed that of the streets as people peacefully moved from one art object to the next.

I wasn't accustomed to the heat of Jerusalem and went to a small hotel, paid my ten shekels and swam. The people there were all Israelis, only Hebrew was heard, but they were not religious. Many Israelis are not religious and even in Jerusalem are very much a part of the complexity of the city.

For me, swimming is relaxing and was a great relief in the heat and matched the mood I felt in the museum. Together these two experiences reflected the ambience of the city. I had a sense of tranquility and peace of mind.

On a bench in a small park near my home, I thought about my mother, how difficult she was, but also how much she loved us even if she was reluctant to be demonstrative or articulate her love.

Somehow, and I don't understand why, the mood of the city on a Sabbath helped me reconcile my mother's erratic characteristics.

Shabbat was ending. It was now sunset and I walked home. Across the courtyard from my balcony, I heard men singing to close the Shabbat. Again, it was the sound of male voices only. Despite my nagging question about the women, I was very calm. Was there something in the air in Jerusalem? In spite of being alone, feeling like an outsider, grieving for my mother, I was at peace. Shabbat Shalom, greetings to the Sabbath.

22

Assignment in India

At two o'clock in the morning, the Bombay (now called Mumbai) airport was alive with activity. Throngs of people were everywhere, sorting and loading their luggage and slowly passing through customs. I came with four enormous pieces of baggage, the largest I could find, all of them heavy with the books I brought to do my work.

I found a rickety luggage carrier, put three pieces on it, dragged the fourth, and slowly, moved outside. The air was hot and wet, with more hordes of people waiting. At the time it seemed as if everyone was screaming for someone.

In this mass confusion, I saw a sign with my name on it, "Dr. Wald." The sign was held by two men who did not speak English, but were able to say, "university." They pointed, picked up my baggage, and I followed.

It was dark and I was alone in the back of the van, with two men who did not speak English, going I did not know where. We rode on and on, through the dark slums of Bombay.

"How long does it take," I asked.

The driver pointed ahead. Through the window I saw people sleeping on mats, on the streets, in the dirt, sights that were so new and strange to me.

Finally, we arrived at the women's dormitory, in India called a hostel. More people helped us into the elevator and took my baggage upstairs. A door opened to my room. In the corner were a small table next to a bed, a chair, and a naked light bulb. In the middle of the floor was a pile of dirt.

A woman spoke to me in English. "You have too much luggage," she said.

I asked about the dirt in the middle of the floor.

"To show you that your room was cleaned," she replied.

I looked around. Two rooms, moldy walls, a ceiling fan in each room. Yes, my own toilet, but where was the water? What was that crawling on the floor? Too large for cockroaches, I thought. Two towels were hanging, I thought they were towels, some kind of harsh, coarse material, washed out several decades ago. The young woman left.

Exhausted, I undressed and tried to put a few things away, but away where? I lay in bed and finally fell asleep. Two hours later I was awakened by noise from the open window and outside my door. It was six in the morning. At home I couldn't stand the heavy tread of my upstairs neighbors. Here the noise overwhelmed me, dogs barking, people screaming, loud voices in the courtyard and outside my door, sounds I couldn't identify.

The young woman of the night before came in.

"Tea? Coffee?" she asked.

"Coffee please."

She brought a pot and some tea biscuits. As I sat and drank I thought to myself, why? Why was I here? What have I done?

But I knew. I came because I was invited, because I seized on all opportunities and took advantage of all adventures. That was the result of moving from dependent wife to accomplished, resourceful, professional woman. I acquired a doctorate, taught in several colleges, and became a specialist in nontraditional higher education for adults. That's why I was there.

This was also an adventure for me, I could learn about a new culture and country very different from the United States. Although bewildered and not yet secure in my abilities in this different world, I was determined to make the most of the opportunity.

The young woman returned.

"Did you sleep well?" she asked.

"What about these cockroaches?"

"We will fix that," she answered. "Would you like more coffee? What do you have in all those suitcases?"

"Books for the work," I replied.

"The Chancellor wants to meet you and I've arranged for you to go at ten this morning. We will take care of the dirt. We will take care of the cockroaches. Do not worry. Tomorrow we will do everything. You have a very nice room, you have screens, you must be someone special," she said.

"How do I take a shower?" I asked.

"Let me show you," the woman said. "This bucket is for taking showers."

"A bucket," I whispered. I was beginning to realize how far from home I was.

"You are most fortunate, you have water in your room. Please I will come for you at 9:30. Do not worry, we will fix everything."

Again I asked myself, what was I doing there? Could I stand it for three months?

When I heard from the Ministry of Education that my application to teach administrators and faculty in India had been accepted, I couldn't quite believe it. Even though I wrote all those proposals, the possibility of finally coming to India seemed remote. But there I was.

That first morning I began to understand that a shower in my room, even a bucket for a shower, was a luxury. And the dirt in the middle of the floor was there to demonstrate that I was cared for. In less than twenty-four hours, I had my first glimpse into the culture of India, a culture with different values, expectations, and practices.

At seven o'clock, the first morning I was in India, I learned how to use the bucket and dressed to meet the Chancellor.

Working in India

The work week was staggering. I was up at five to prepare for the day. The college library had no books I could use. Although I brought suitcases of books, I often had to scrounge around for what I needed. The American Center was sometimes useful, but books on education were hard to find anywhere.

I was a specialist in higher education for adults and that was the principal reason I was invited. The members of the class were faculty and administrators from S.N.D.T, the university that was my principal assignment, and Bombay University. They all had a master's degree and some a Doctorate. They were mature, with families of their own.

The class met three days a week from 3:30 p.m. to 6:30 p.m., and every other week we went on a field trip for the fourth day. The time between ten and teaching was spent in the office, attending staff meetings, supervising student projects, meeting individually and in small groups, and searching for resources. On Saturdays, we worked from 10 a.m. to 1 p.m.

The director of this program was an esteemed educator from Great Britain, and I was his co-chair. The demands never stopped. In addition to working directly with this post-graduate program I was asked to "Prepare a training program." "Write a women's studies curriculum." "Meet with the women's studies research staff." "Go to Poona to lead a training program for teachers."

At first I was perplexed by the authoritarian demands. At Empire State College, deans and administrators would consult with you regarding requests for special projects. I learned this was a different world; authority was fundamental in this culture and no one questioned anything, at least openly. At the same time, the people I worked with were invested in a democratic vision and what they could do in their roles as educators for adults. Life and work in India were certainly perplexing at times.

At first, I was overwhelmed by the work demands but gradually learned to take it in stride. Slowly, the dark circles under my eyes got lighter. I was amazed by my own ability to be calm, energetic, and productive. I was even interviewed on radio and by the local newspaper regarding women's issues and was getting to be something of a celebrity. At home no one knew me.

*

The issues of the language of education in India make the problems of bilingualism in the United States seem easy to resolve. The official language of India is Hindi, while English is the language of the universities, which is related to the British presence for so many years. Then there are the local dialects, hundreds of them that are an important part of the culture. Each university is committed to teaching in the mother tongue of that region.

There are two mother tongues in the area of the university where I was working and courses were offered in Mujarti, Guyarti, Hindi and English. Students could not always communicate with each other, and often students and teachers do not speak the same language. I was continually floored by this notion of multiple languages. Although several of the members of our program were tentative with English, our program was designed in English. I was never sure who understood me and who didn't.

The third week I was there I was asked to open a training program preceded by a ceremony. Rituals are intrinsic to everyday life here. My speech was translated into Mujarti, the mother tongue of this area. I had a feeling that maybe I was at a United Nations meeting. Everything was so new and unexpected.

*

One day we went on a field trip to the Family Planning Association of India. The theme of the presentation was sterilization. When I innocently asked who was sterilized, the men or the women, everyone laughed. In the rural villages, we were told, there were condom distribution centers. Even after two months in India, my imagination could not grasp how the condoms were distributed—by request, rotation, corruption, or lottery? Who would venture a guess in India? Every day there was at least one surprise. And I finally began to comprehend that in India, all the rituals and activities of daily life that we take for granted in the United States were complicated. Education regarding the activities of daily living was a necessity.

*

After much planning, I visited a literacy program for adults in a rural Indian village. I boarded a train at 6:45 a.m. to meet Hema. At that time Hema was a social worker in the adult education department at Bombay University. One of her responsibilities was supervising the adult reading program in the villages.

We planned to meet at a station about one-half hour from central

Bombay. Hema waited for me on the station platform wearing an impeccably ironed sari. She was so beautiful, a perfectly round face, classic features, and the usual red dot on her forehead. She was six months pregnant.

We traveled by two trains, two buses, and an auto-rickshaw. The trip took two and a half hours and was bumpy. I didn't understand how Hema stood it, I had a queasy stomach. "She could lose the baby on this trip," I thought.

The reading program she supervised was connected to a college two hours from Bombay. She explained that all students were responsible for working either in a reading program or some other community service activity. We were going to visit a student who was teaching reading to adults. I asked about training. There was a two-day workshop on methods of teaching reading. Since I taught methods for teaching reading in a teacher education setting, I wondered how it was possible to train people in such a short time, but I tried to keep an open mind.

Nothing prepared me for this visit. The ground was barren, just dirt and huts spread out as far as the eye could see. Illiteracy is a problem in the United States too, but even in the most disadvantaged areas, there are street signs, numbers on houses, newspapers, and television programs with print. This was a totally non-print society, not a sign around, not a book, not a number, not a newspaper, and, perhaps, not a reason for learning to read.

In this village, reading was considered women's work and attendance at the lessons was erratic. As we approached the village, the women and their children began to gather in a central place on a wooden platform. The materials used in that reading lesson were developed by a major adult education university, cost many thousands of dollars and were about the mouth and teeth. These stories were totally irrelevant to the needs and experiences of this

Indian village. There was one book for every four people. Each person read a few sentences in turn. No new words were introduced or skills explained. The children sat quietly, their eyes on me, I was the stranger. When the lesson was over, the teacher collected the books and put them in her bag, no books remained when she left.

At four o'clock, I was exhausted and could not go on, but Hema had another village to visit. We took a bus together and after an hour separated, she went on to the next village, and I went back to Bombay. She did this twice a month. I worried about her pregnancy and asked her how she felt. "Not too good," she replied, "but they are waiting for me in the next place."

The next day, I called the university to thank Hema, but she did not come to work for three days. She had no phone. On the fourth day, she returned. I bought a gift for her baby and left it with a friend. She gave me a farewell gift. Back home, months later, I received a thank you note, her baby boy was fine.

*

Field trips were essential components of this graduate program. On one trip we visited the Bombay Center. During the time I was in India, the Bombay Society for Adult Education had centers all through the city, in railroad stations, on the streets, in the open areas. Twenty-five thousand students were enrolled. Programs for adults boggled the mind. Their creativity without resources deserve respect.

On a field trip, we visited an educational TV station where the director of the Bombay Society talked to us about his work. He began his career as a teacher and developed radio programs for agricultural workers. Eventually, he moved to TV and at that time was the producer of two thirty-minute programs a week from which five hundred and twenty clubs were formed. He tried to visit all the clubs and functioned with a staff of one. He also wrote a monthly newsletter. He gave me a copy, but it was in Hindi.

"My wife is always angry," he told us. "She complains that I am never home and work too hard." But he was totally committed to bringing education to as many people as he could no matter what sacrifices he had to make.

This visit reinforced for me again that the vision of democracy through education was a natural everyday conversation here. I felt ennobled by the work, the people, and their commitment to their country.

*

In addition to my regular job, I was required by the grant to consult with the president of the new Open University and his faculty in New Delhi. My background at Empire Sate College was my credential. Numbers here stagger the mind. In ten years they anticipated five million students in five thousand centers around the country. During the day we discussed all aspects of an open university plan—credits for life experience, experimental curriculum design, issues for working with an adult population, and credentials for faculty.

Continuing the conversation which went on all day, at night we had dinner at the country club where the waiting list for membership was eighteen years at that time. I was the only woman. They asked if I was married. I answered, "Yes, of course," and everyone was relieved, including me. Divorce was difficult for them to understand so if I was asked I simply said, "Yes, I am married."

The Director told me proudly that there was one female member on the faculty, although she was not there the week I visited. I told them they were trying to fool me, she was really a phantom. They looked at me sideways, not quite sure how to answer. Was I serious or joking?

My work in India changed me. I learned that adult education was much more than immersing oneself in history or English or some other academic discipline. It had to do with several fundamental aspects of living—literacy, population control, and democracy. The people I worked with were pioneers in a country where class designations had been a way of life. They were committed to changing this vast, complex country to a place where people had opportunities never before envisioned. I felt invigorated and proud to be part, however small a part, of that process.

Images and Impressions

In the newspaper, I read that 63,000 babies are born every day in India. 25,000 die each day.

Little girls with babies on their hips were on every street corner near the university. They were begging.

Children were on the street all day and night. It was evident that there was no compulsory schooling here.

I saw a line of children, ages approximately three to twelve, patiently waiting near a closed door. It was a bread distribution line and each child received a large loaf and ran off.

Women took their children everywhere. I bought bananas from a woman on the street, she sat on the pavement cross-legged, her basket in front of her on the sidewalk. A baby slept in her lap.

Child labor was part of the order of life here. In the factories children from six years old were working. People lived in the streets with their families, their pots, their household goods. They have the same spot everyday, never leave it.

Walking across an open field one morning, I saw street people brushing their teeth from a tin. A man was washing his feet.

Men walked together in the streets holding hands. Men and women never touch or show any sign of affection in public.

A man at the university always wore a hat. He shaved his head in mourning for his father.

Everyone in India seemed to have bad teeth, black, crooked, missing teeth, even in the highest circles.

A funeral procession passed near the hostel, all men, women were not permitted.

Two of the factories I visited outside of Jaipur were open seven days a week. People were only paid for the days they worked, ten rupees a day, about ninety cents, no weekends, holidays, or vacations.

I needed something typed. Down the street was a secretarial service, the man typed outside with an IBM electric typewriter, connected to a long extension wire that went inside.

Across the street, a man made sandals. I give him a print of my sister, Milly's foot and in a week they were ready. They fit her perfectly.

All of Bombay appeared to be polluted, the streets, the water, the air.

The noise was constant, very few traffic lights, and I took a chance crossing the street because like the British, cars were driven on the left. I never became accustomed to this reversal and often stepped off the curb, looked the wrong way, and narrowly missed getting hit.

The train system was inherited from the British, and for a country that runs on inefficiency, the train system was remarkably reliable. In the downtown station in Bombay, near the university, a train arrived and left every three minutes.

Some people traveled one-and-a-half to three hours each way to work.

Sometimes I thought this was not real life, this was a movie, people hanging from the sides of trains, bodies hanging from the doors, and not one more body could fit in.

I was advised to always travel second class, all women. First-class is mixed, men and women, and it might be dangerous for me.

Bombay was in a housing crisis and has been for generations. People cannot marry as they have no place to live.

Many of the buildings were shored up with stilts, it was anticipated that two hundred and forty buildings would collapse this year during the monsoon season.

In Bombay, water was a preoccupation and an occupation. A few of the wealthy apartment houses had huge water tanks on their roofs where water was collected during the rainy season.

Most people in Bombay waited for the distribution from the main water system. Water was distributed around the clock, some people received it at two a.m., others at four, and so on.

People also kept huge buckets filled with water all the time. Even though water was rationed, there were some days when there was no water at all. The filled buckets were put to good use.

In the hostel much time was spent in ironing saris, and there was a large room for this.

The students came to my room often. "Do I have American tapes of rock and roll? Do I know how to dance the rock and roll?"

The weather was hot and wet. All the walls were moldy. My room was painted just before I came, but the rest of the dormitory looked dingy and dirty from the dampness.

Two faculty members shared the room next to me. One was unmarried, and said "I will not marry for a dowry." The other was married for five years, her husband lived in Agra because they could not find jobs in the same city.

The weather was another major preoccupation, at least for me. Often, I would get up exhausted, with dark circles under my eyes. The heat and humidity were almost unbearable.

I'm a New Yorker, used to the fast pace. If nothing else, I've learned patience here. Sometimes, to shower and dress were monumental tasks.

We take so many things for granted back home, a telephone call without static or interruption, books, screens, water, air-conditioning, television, leisure time, fun, cleanliness.

When you went to the post office to mail a letter you stood in three lines, one to get your letter weighed, two to get your stamp, three to get it postmarked. When I asked, "Wouldn't it be better to have three lines all doing the three functions?" Someone answered, "Then you would need three scales." The arrogance of Americans.

I have fallen in love with India.

23

Unfinished Business

I went half-way around the world to the most unlikely setting you can imagine to settle my unfinished business. I always wore so many hats, completing the doctorate, forging a career, parenting, crafting a personal life. Unfinished business has dogged me all my adult life, bills to be paid, articles to be written, issues to be resolved with the children.

In the Spring of 1988, when I worked in Israel, my friend, Muriel, and I signed up for a seven-day camping trip to the Sinai and down the coast of Egypt. We went on an adventure trip, but when I returned home I realized what a complex journey it turned out to be. In just a few days in the Sinai, some new ideas and insights changed my thinking dramatically.

As luck would have it, just before we were due to leave, I came down with a bad bladder infection. The doctor prescribed a strong antibiotic and told me to drink lots of water on the trip. "You will be fine," he said.

We crossed the border into Egypt at Eilat and met our companions, a

Norwegian man who worked with the United Nations in Lebanon, an Italian man, and six Germans, three men and three women. Our guide, Chris, was from Belgium and he had two Egyptian assistants. English was the one language we had in common. Muriel and I were the only people over thirty-five.

Our transportation and shelter for the entire trip was a bulky Mercedes bus-jeep with huge tires, the kind you see on American trailer trucks, necessary to get through deep sand, a rack for storage, water tanks with two spigots built into the truck and very hard seats. Later as we drove long distances, I was aware of the soreness in my left side, probably my infected bladder, from the bumps.

On that first long bus ride and during our picnic lunch, I began to get acquainted with the other people. I couldn't pinpoint it exactly, but I felt slightly uneasy, and off-balance.

Never before had I been with so many Germans at one time. They were outgoing young people and I was intrigued by their love of travel and their accents as they spoke English. These young, fun-loving people were a sharp contrast to my memories of the Second World War and the killing of six million Jews.

World War II took place over sixty years ago and many people I know still will not go to Germany. I have never been there either except once in the Frankfurt airport changing planes. The memories of the War and the Holocaust are as vivid as if those events happened yesterday. My father provided necessary money and affidavits for many Jewish people to come to the United States. Many of my male friends served in the armed forces, and several of them never came back. The atrocities of that time are still sharp for many of us. For me, it was complicated to connect these happy, fun-loving young travelers on the bus with the history of that period.

The Intifada (the periodic struggle between Israelis and Palestinians) in Israel began that previous December, and although tourism was off, the Germans still came in hordes, traveling to all the Christian sights. It was ironic that in times of stress for Israel, the Germans were helping the sorely depressed economy.

For several hours on the bus that first day, I sat next to Christine, one of the German girls. She was twenty-five and worked in her father's haberdashery shop in Munich. He was in the Second World War. I asked her about the Jewish star around her neck.

"I traveled through Israel, and everyone there wears one." she told me. I stared at her but didn't say a word.

She was completely unconscious about the meaning of that star. I wondered what would happen when this young woman went home with this "memento" around her neck. Her family might remember other Stars of David sewed to clothing. Or, perhaps they had forgotten, and that was why Christine knew nothing about this history.

Chris, our leader, said the Sinai was his favorite place in the world. He wouldn't tell us why, we needed to find out for ourselves. In a very few hours, I began to get a glimmer of what he meant. We were transfixed by large plains of loose sand, high mountains and rock formations. I imagined the desert as this wide expanse of sand with an occasional dune or hill, but the Sinai was anything but flat, and dried brush and trees dotted the landscape.

Our first stop was a wide wadi, a dried up riverbed. For three hours, we climbed massive, smooth rocks and descended deep crevasses. We went from one mountain crest to the next, climbing up one side and going down the other. It was difficult for me as I puffed up the inclines, drinking water, with all those antibiotics and the hot desert sun.

I understood why this hike was first on our schedule. We were getting to know the desert, experiencing first-hand the vagaries, diversity, obstacles, and beauty Chris alluded to earlier in the day.

When we finished, I was exhausted. But there was the challenge, and it was fun. If I had been feeling well, I would have enjoyed every minute of it. And now, regardless of age, illness, swollen ankles, and the hot desert sun, I wanted to do it. After all, it was another peak to be conquered, another thing to accomplish.

Our first overnight stop, St. Catherine's, was a campsite set at the foot of Mt. Sinai. In the tent, platforms were lined up side by side, we each took one, stretched out our sleeping bags, and put our clothes at the foot. The desert, so hot in the day, was freezing now in the night, high up in the mountains. This night was breathtaking, the sky a blanket of stars, so close, you felt as if you could put your hand out and touch them, a roof of nature. In the middle of the night it was beautiful, shadowy, with the pale light coming over the mountains and the stars glistening. More and more I understood Chris's love of this mysterious, complex Sinai.

The plan was to get up at three a.m. to climb Mt. Sinai for two-and-a half hours to reach the crest at sun-up, and relive the place and time when Moses received the tablets with the Ten Commandments. The climb sounded difficult, maybe I wouldn't go. My friend, Muriel said, "How can you miss it?" And she was right. Of course, I would go.

At three a.m. we were awakened. Cold and tired, my ankles still swollen, I really didn't want to climb Mt. Sinai. The Italian man sleeping on the left of me did not get up.

"I may be crazy," he said, "but I'm not stupid."

His refusal gave me permission not to go. I watched the others, all these non-Jews preparing for the long climb in the middle of the night in the middle of the Sinai, while I, the Jew, elected to stay and sleep. I understood why they wanted to go, their excitement. But I had difficulty reconciling their eagerness and their energy with the Holocaust. Were these people from the same country? After they left to do the climb, I thought about the dilemma I felt about these vivacious young Germans. I realized that even my own children did not really understand this period of history.

They returned in late morning, tired and exhilarated. They had reached the peak just at sun-up to relive the story of Moses and the Ten Commandments. The Jewish people do not believe this story; the place where Moses received the Ten Commandments is unknown. I was relieved that I didn't go

We took off again in our bumpy bus. After some distance, we left the road and now spent all our time driving through the Sinai. At one point, we stopped to let air out of the tires, which was the only way to get through the deep sand. Sometimes we got out of the bus and walked.

We saw Bedouins and wadis and crevasses and every kind of mountain and rock formation one might imagine. We saw writings on stones and graveyards from the Bronze Age. We were asked to collect wood, dried cactus, sticks. "Tie them up in bundles for the night," Chris said.

We were the only people around. The silence was grand, mysterious, and unfamiliar. It was hard to imagine that Moses and the Jewish people roamed this land for forty years. How did they live? What did they eat? How did they protect themselves, from the wind and the sun?

Finally, we made camp for the night in another huge wadi between two mountains. We built a fire with the wood collected that afternoon, dinner was started, including soup, we drank wine and eventually vodka to keep warm.

Chris, our guide, talked and led us in wonderful conversation. He told us about the mystery of the Sinai and its forever changing forms. He talked of other deserts, but this one was special. Just the night before, we'd been strangers, and now, in the wadi, with the stars and wind whistling, we knew each other, strangers from so many places, now community here in the Sinai. But that night, I became conscious of other levels of unfinished business, the complexity of the political world, the Sinai, so close to Israel, Egypt and Israel, Germans and Jews.

Muriel and I put our sleeping bags together, we needed each other in this alien world. In the middle of the night, the desert wind began, a howling, freezing, never-ending cold current of air that penetrated my sleeping bag, my body, my soul. It even penetrated the woolen sweater the Norwegian loaned me. He lived in the northern part of Norway and this sweater kept him warm when he slept in the snow. But not in the desert. There, the wind howled right through the sweater. I was so cold I didn't know how I would make it to morning.

Henrik, a young man about thirty, was sleeping near me. Also awake, he said, "This is the worst night of my life. The sleeping bags are like paper."

I agreed.

About five in the morning, we began to get up. It was wonderful watching the sun come up over the mountains. The beauty took my breath away. Not too long ago I thought I would never be warm again, but the temperature changes quickly in the desert.

Another long hike was on the agenda for the morning. Even Chris didn't try to persuade me. He could see that my eyes and ankles were swollen, I looked so tired. I got water from the spigots on the bus and went out into the desert to wash and change my clothes. There I was, nude, in this great expanse of the Sinai, alone, marveling at nature, the beauty of the silence; the cold was worth this moment. It was wonderful to contemplate that Moses might have stood in this very spot.

But my side was hurting, my ankles were swollen, and the guide, Chris, could not promise warmth for the next night, only the night after the next on our way to Sharm El Sheik. He said I could get a ride back to Eilat at our next stop, but not after that, I must decide.

Should I go, should I stay? How could I leave this wondrous place, this new experience? I wanted to see Sharm El Sheik, to go snorkeling in its warm waters. I changed my mind a million times.

Those old feelings of unfinished business, so many things to do, to fix to accomplish, to resolve, so many challenges, new experiences not to be missed. How could I leave?

Finally, reason took over, and I decided to return home.

On the long ride back to Eilat I glanced at myself in the rear-view mirror of the bus. I looked old and haggard. When I looked down, I saw my legs were still puffy.

The bus drove back along a road that paralleled the Red Sea. The sea was beautiful, calm, aqua in color. The last few days were on my mind, the beauty that I witnessed, the cold I tried to conquer, the paradoxical images of Germans and Jews; Germans traveling through Israel, climbing mountains at three o'clock in the morning to see the place where Moses came, the Jewish star around the young girl's neck.

What prepared me for this—for finding myself in an alien mysterious world? I would have liked to stay, perhaps I should have stayed, could I forgive myself for not? Did I fail some gigantic test? But the dangers were real, the cold, the pain on my left side, the wind. Were the other dangers real? The mystery and unpredictability of nature, the unknown, the howling of the wind, being in a world that had been hostile to Jews.

At the customs in Eilat, the Egyptians were solemn, serious and bureaucratic. The customs inspector searched through my luggage, studied my David Shippler book, *Arab and Jew*, and stared at me. Finally, I walked across to the Israeli side. The customs there, "shalom," laughter, "here sit down, welcome, shalom, shalom." I was home.

On the long bus ride back to Jerusalem I reflected on some unfinished business in the Sinai Desert. The Sinai was so beautiful, I would have liked to see it all. Perhaps I will go back, I probably won't. It doesn't matter because there is all that other unfinished business to make sense of and comprehend, new chapters to be written, men and women, Jews and Germans, Egypt and Israel.

Unfinished business has haunted me all my life. There were all those other tests that I didn't take. Should I have found some approach for reconciling with my father? Were there possibilities for climbing the career ladder I might have pursued? Why did I never remarry? Could I have averted my brother's suicide? How?

On the long ride back to Eilat that day I also realized some issues were beyond my control. I don't know how I could have prevented the physical problem that forced me to leave the camping trip. I could not repair my parents' difficulties, they had to do that for themselves. No matter how hard you try, not everything can be finished or resolved I know that now.

24

Disappointing Moves

My house in Great Neck, New York, was more than a house. It was a haven for more than twenty-five years, a place of life and love, laughing and crying. This house was a metaphor for growing—a place where my children and I grew up.

In that house, I had three different lives: the life of a young wife and parent, then the second life as a single working mother, and finally, after my children had grown and left, the life of the empty nest, the place in which I lived with friends, with my lover, and always with my work.

So many people passed through that house and through our lives and gave meaning to who we were and what we became—my parents, my brothers and sister, my ex-husband, friends who cared for me during the divorce, the women who cared for my children while I studied and worked, my children, the men in my life, and me. It was also dingy, always needing repairs, painting, fixing something or other. But for me, the house was beautiful. Yet, time brings change.

The children were gone, living their own lives, and I felt isolated living alone in that big house.

"Sell the house," everyone said. "This is a good time, the market is high, change your life."

Maybe it will change my luck, I thought. What do I need it for? Now's the time. Richard and I just ended our long relationship. The house was worth a small fortune, or so it seemed then. And it was time for a change, from what to what, I wasn't sure, but indeed time for a change.

I moved to an apartment, bought new furniture, comfortable, chic, and graceful. After all those years of taking care of everything, I found the luxury of security, not having to fix things myself, the freedom not to worry, to come home at night, safe, and secure, not troubled by broken burners, squirrels in the roof, leaky plumbing, a possible intruder.

I missed the big empty rooms, the place to iron, the basement to store things, the rooms for my grandchildren. Here, I heard the noises of my neighbors, had to park my car a million miles away, struggled with bundles, climbed the stairs. I missed my roots, my walls, and the place where my children grew up, the quiet street. I did the same things at home now, read, wrote, had friends in, my family came to visit. But somehow I felt cramped in the spaces of my soul.

25

The Passover Seder: A Search for Freedom

When I was a child, I wasn't exactly sure what Passover meant. Every year I heard the same story; Moses freed the Jewish slaves and led them out of Egypt. They roamed the desert for forty years, received the Ten Commandments and, finally, reached Israel. The ancient Passover story meant freedom for the Jews, freedom to leave slavery, freedom to leave Egypt, freedom to find the Promised Land.

The Seder is literally a reenactment or story of the Jewish experience, the years of bondage in slavery, the search for freedom, the forty years of wandering to reach "the Promised Land." Today, I know it is a metaphor for freedom, but then I didn't know where Egypt was or what was meant by the Promised Land.

In my earliest memories, my grandfather led the Seder. He was a gentle man, small in stature, with a soft voice. He would read in Hebrew, from the Haggadah, the book describing ritual, the men sometimes joining, while everyone else, the women and children, sat around the table, waiting and listening. My uncle took over after my grandfather died. No one translated the Hebrew and I don't know if my grandfather or uncle really understood what they were reading. But the meal was fun because it was family-centered.

A pivotal moment in the Seder ritual originates with a child asking the four questions. At eight, I began Hebrew school and could read the questions in Hebrew and English, beginning with "Why is this night different from all other nights?"

The remainder of the Passover meal is a response to these questions, the meaning of Passover, the rituals and the special food. The central themes are freedom—what is freedom, who is free?

After Charly and I were married, we had our own Seders. As the woman of the house, I took on my mother's role, shopping, cleaning, cooking, and getting the table ready. My husband always led these Seders. At our Seders we used children's Haggadahs, the English translation was right there with the Hebrew and the children could understand the holiday.

One Seder stands out. All Charly's family came from upper New York State. He was the youngest of five, so there were many aunts and uncles. My children had seventeen cousins. Charly and his three brothers were all in the armed services during the Second World War, which set the stage for talking about that time, the reasons for the war and what happened since. We made sure to talk about the meaning of freedom in a way that the children could understand and remember.

After the divorce, I continued the Seders and over time, my own voice evolved depending on where I was in my life and what questions I had about freedom. I led them and always ended with: "What is freedom, who is enslaved, who is free?"

For some of those Seders, Richard, my long-time lover, and I led them together. All our children, his and mine, relatives, and friends came. First, we invited ten people, then fifteen, once even twenty. We were so proud, so steeped in promise. Our Seders were contemporary, based on themes about the Holocaust, Anne Frank, poverty in America, Vietnam, and civil rights. We always ended with: "What is freedom, who is enslaved, who is free?

Another year, again alone, it was the Feminist Seder, the liberation of women, our mothers, our daughters, ourselves; a reflection of my status, my identity, my friends, my world. God was She. I led this Seder as a symbol of my own freedom. The four sons were transformed into four daughters. We talked of Sarah, Rachel, Miriam, Leah, the matriarchs. The men were uneasy reading God as She, all the women smiled.

The year I lived in Israel directing a unit of my college, I gained a new perspective on the Seder. People there were obsessed with removing bread from their homes, which was considered a symbol of the residue of slavery. In the desert, only matzoh, unleavened bread, and a staple of the Passover feast, was eaten.

Alice, my friend and colleague, told me, "Everything must be cleaned for Passover."

Cleaning out the "chametz," the bread, was necessary even for her car. For three days in a row she went to the carwash but could not stand the lines. On the fourth day, the final one before the holiday, she waited in line for two hours and came late to work with her car clean and shining.

Alice emigrated from England and loved living in Israel, but was particularly sad that year because one daughter had recently moved to Australia and her other children were in England. She asked if I would go with her to the home of friends who had no other family.

"Yes, of course, I would go." I brought flowers. I, too, missed my family and wore my mother's earrings, a connection to my home.

The small apartment was clean, the yearly dishes set, and my flowers were the centerpiece. Alice's friend worked all week to prepare, clean the house, shop and cook. Her three sons helped, one twelve, one eight, and one eighteen on leave from the army for the holiday.

The father had returned just that day from the United States where he had gone to earn some money. Everyone had Haggadahs and read quietly in Hebrew the way I remember my grandfather and uncle reading. This Seder was long and literal, with little conversation.

The strain was palpable. The father sat stiffly as the sons furtively glanced at the man whom they had not seen for six months. The mother waited, hoping he would say how well she looked, that the sons were also well, the table beautiful, and the food delicious.

Instead, all he said was, "What did you do to your hair?"

She replied, "You're rushing through the Seder."

The door was opened to embrace Elijah, the ancient prophet, the symbol of hospitality to strangers. Who were the real strangers in this house, in this family?

"We did a good deed," Alice said on our way home. "We kept the conversation going, helped with their awkwardness, their estrangement, their shyness with each other."

In Israel, Passover is a way of life, it takes over the country. In the United States that I know, Passover is a Jewish ritual, but does not have the same intensity as the religious holiday in Israel. But this Seder in Israel reminded me of the Seders of my childhood and marriage, the readings, the lack of understanding, the lack of explanations, the tension between my parents, the unspoken tension between my husband and me, and the emotional desert into which I was pushed after the divorce.

That Seder in Israel crystallized for me both the misery and possibilities of marriage and reawakened all the turning points in my own journey—the trauma of divorce, single parenting, the ups and downs of several relationships, the steps to get to this new place, a professional, working, accomplished, traveling and living alone in another country, finding my inner core, my creativity, my own voice.

My marriage began in full bloom, but slowly over time it felt quite barren. Just as the Jewish people had been slaves, I had been captive in the notion of what my role was, what I had to do and how to do it. What is freedom? Who is free? Free from what? "Living happily ever after" was an unfulfilled promise.

The marriage ended, and I began a new journey, a journey sometimes frightening and, often, lonely. Like the Jewish people wandering in the desert, I went out into the world with my children and wandered for a long time without a clear understanding of where I wanted to go or my final destination. What was my Promised Land? Eventually, my career evolved, I acquired a doctorate and was one of the first faculty members at a new experimental college. And I had new relationships. Richard and I were together for almost twelve years and both the strengths and limitations of this relationship helped me forge a new voice for myself.

As I left that Seder in Israel, I missed my family, my children, my center, my Promised Land. Paradoxically, I left that Seder feeling free, free in a strange land.

Back in the United States, I came into my own. Now, in my own home, my own Seders, I wrote my own Haggadah. The table is set with all my beautiful things, my dishes, my mother's silver, glasses collected from my travels, candlesticks from Sweden, my sister's flowers. I like tradition, I like the modern world.

Family and friends, people read prayers and poetry, talk about their lives, their journeys, their own quests for freedom, the freedom of the Jews, the exodus of the Soviet Jews, each from our own Exodus, our particular bondage.

The years pass, and the Seders go on and on. Each one is different and yet all the same. We talk together about all the themes of the

Passover Seder—modern plagues, Aids, poverty, war, violence, and the freedom and problems of living in a modern democracy, America. We have reached the Promised Land, a land where freedom roams, the desert blooms, and my family thrives.

Each year we ask, "What is freedom, who is enslaved, who is free?" I am here, this is my voice.

Working in India — 1985

Working in Israel — 1987

As Time Goes By

Circa 1970's

Circa 1980's

Circa 1990's

Current Photo

PART 5

Resolution

Illness and death also reinforces the idea that life matters, and each day is important.

26

Things Matter

I have more stuff than I will ever need, but I love all of it. I have things from my grandparents, my mother, my travels, my friends, and my family. They are treasured memories.

I love the pieces my children gave me; a deep-green Mexican tequila decanter and lovely pink and white pottery with matching salt and pepper shakers. I love the music box from my long-time friends Beverly and Sam that plays the melody, "Memories." My mother's big pot is perfect for cooking barbecue sauce or soup or corn. The cover doesn't fit too tightly, but I remember all the treats—sweet and sour stuffed cabbage, meat balls, and chicken soup with matzoh balls—that came out of that pot. How could I possibly give it away?

In 1972 I went to Israel and bought a vase for forty-two cents from a Bedouin on a camel. That vase has sat on a shelf in all the places I've lived. And that wonderful sculpture of mother and child by an Ethiopian Jewish artist I bought in a crafts fair in Jerusalem is on the next shelf.

My sister, Milly, died several years ago, and I have her warm, cuddly, over-sized robe, her sweater which is miles too big for me, and her blue and white dishes. When I wear her clothes I feel close to her. I savor drinking coffee from Milly's mugs and eating dinner from her dishes. Each meal is a reminder of her. At night, watching television, I wear her black velvet very big for me caftan. Some of her needlepoint hangs in my home, crowding the walls, but where else could it all go?

My bureau drawers are filled with things I never use like my Aunt Dotty's earrings and my mother's pins. Her diamond ring is in the vault. My sister loved big rhinestone-covered pins, all of which I have, some in the bureau, some in a box under the kitchen table. Looking through my closet, preparing for winter, I found all the fur collars she put on different coats and dresses and her wonderful art deco gloves with rhinestones and fur—things my low-key Boston friends would think are tacky.

Many people I know are downsizing at this stage of life. They move from big houses to smaller condominiums or townhouses. The collected wisdom is that older people don't need much, which I don't go along with at all. I want all my "stuff" around me for as long as I live. I remember when my precious Aunt Dotty was in an assisted-living residence in Florida. She was stripped down to a few photographs; other things she wanted to keep were often stolen. She was totally paralyzed for the last ten years of her life, and I know seeing those things around her would have been comforting. Why don't the planners of these developments understand that people need their memories and symbols of the meaning of their lives?

I have four desks in my apartment. They are not all desks, but I use them as if they were. There is the computer desk on which I can never find the room to do anything else but use the computer. The desk in my bedroom is where I pay my bills. The kitchen table is where all the catalogs from museums, ballet, and theater are stored.

Here I keep Verizon ads, paper clips, napkin holders, and everything else that I don't know what to do with. The dining room table becomes a desk for working on special projects like the next session for a course I am teaching, the essays for this book, or the folder with the blinds I am ordering for the dining room windows, and the lovely plate my friend, Pat gave me. I could never give that away because I keep all presents forever.

In my last move, four years ago, I gave away three hundred and fifty books. Recently I needed two of them for an article I am writing. So I am not giving away books ever again. They will all be with me, I hope, until I die.

I always say I am going to organize my family pictures into albums, but of course I never do. I have three boxes of them stored on the top shelf of my bedroom closet and under the bed. I have some photographs I don't even recognize. My children definitely will not want them, although maybe they'll want some of the tons of pictures I have of them growing up. I once made an album for each one, but I still have many more. And now I have pictures of all those grandchildren at every year of their lives. What will happen to them all?

And what about all those things I have written over the years? I have a box of poetry that is so big it will not fit on any shelf or under the bed and now sits under the desk in the bedroom. I still have papers from Empire State College, letters of recommendation, my tenure papers from 1972, all the grants and reports—why do I keep them? I suppose because they help me relive all the different struggles, accomplishments, and times of my life. And my dissertation, I have two copies. That was, indeed, a struggle but also a great achievement for me.

Sometimes when I visit other people's homes I wonder, "Where is everything?" I visited an old friend recently, a former colleague, when I went to New York. I didn't see the old newspapers, the magazines waiting for a pause in life to be read, the reading glasses. There wasn't a glimpse of mail waiting to be answered or any books stuffed into crowded bookcases. How does she do it? The order troubles me. Where are the symbols of a lifetime—things, photographs, and books half-read?

One of the hardest things for me is clothes. My closets are packed with things I haven't worn in years. There is the jacket I wore to my cousin's son's wedding, and he now has a fifteen-year-old daughter. Some coats I have not worn since I moved to Boston ten years ago. My daughter, Beth, tells me that if she has not worn something in a year out it goes. Where does she get the courage?

Sometimes I think it is courage, other times I fantasize that I will one day be thin again and wear a size six dress. But most of all, clothes also rekindle memories. I still have the dress I wore to Marian's wedding, she was married in 1980. I shortened the dress from full-to below the knee and wore it again to Beth's wedding, thirteen years later. It is more than just a dress. It is *the wedding dress,* there are memories embedded in its creases.

I have a collection of all my old passports. They remind me of all the places I have been and when. In one drawer of my mother's chest I have all my old glasses. I can't see out of any of them, my prescriptions have changed many times, but I don't throw them away. Why? I have no idea; maybe I keep them as reminders of times past. Anyway, they seem cozy in the bottom of one drawer or another.

What would I take if I had to leave my home for some emergency? If there was some cataclysmic event like a fire, I would only be able to take small things that I could carry. Photographs would be the best resource for memories. Of course, I would take different photographs of my family. I could not leave my sister behind or my mother or brother or Marcia, his wife, or their children. I would need to remember my friends and take their photos, too. I would take what I could to put under a pillow wherever I slept. Those pictures could keep me warm forever.

27

Worry

Today we are having an "almost" blizzard. The snow began falling last night and the reports indicate that we may have up to twenty inches of snow by tomorrow. My son needed to fly home from California, and scheduled a flight for today. When I heard the weather report, I began to worry how he would get home. Fortunately, he changed to a flight last night and arrived this morning, but with a fever of 102 degrees. So I am still worried. Why didn't he take the flu shot? How will he get to the doctor if he needs to? If the fever turns into pneumonia, it would be his second bout in five years. No wonder I worry.

My oldest grandson came home last night because his girlfriend's father is suddenly in the hospital. How will he get back to school for his finals? He didn't bring boots, will he catch pneumonia? His brother, Justin, stayed overnight with a friend from school. Marian, my daughter and his mother, drove to Hamilton to pick him up. That is the area which, so far, has the most snow, almost eight inches already. This causes me great worry.

At six in the morning, my other daughter, Beth, opened the health club she and her husband own. She is going to close the club at noon, but then how will she get home?

"Don't worry Mom," she says, "I know what I am doing, I have it all under control."

And how come she is opening the club? What about him? I worry that I can't help her. She is, after all, forty-five, and can take care of herself.

My granddaughter is supposed to go to the Senior Cotillion in her school in the midst of this storm tonight. I worry even though I am sure it will be canceled.

The woman upstairs is away, and her daughter left at 7:30 a.m. to take the SAT's. How will she get home? She was wearing a skimpy jacket. Did she have boots? She left despite my prediction that the test would be cancelled, but I couldn't convince her. I seem to worry about children everywhere, mine, my grandchildren, and other people's.

My brother's oldest daughter lives in Charlotte, North Carolina, and is in great difficulty, emotionally and financially. She has two daughters by two husbands and really neglects them. She lost one daughter in a custody battle. My brother taught the older daughter to drive so she could get to school. My niece does not care about getting her to school. I worry about her daughter driving everyday, but she is sixteen and sixteen is legal in North Carolina. I also worry about my brother worrying about her. I don't want him to have a heart attack.

In the midst of this freezing spell, Todd, my grandson, who had pneumonia, is back at school having to walk across the yard for meals. It is nine degrees there. He does not like to wear a coat, has a virus, and is coughing. I speak to my daughter, "maybe we should go and get him."

"No," she says, "he has to learn to take care of himself."

Although she worries too, she is steadfast in her opinion, and I think to myself, is this the time to teach him a lesson? I worry about her ideas about parenting and Todd being alone up there.

Jonathan, my-fifteen-year-old grandson, has his second bout with strep throat in less than a month. Do I need to repeat how that worries me?

I read in the *Boston Globe* that people with H-Pylori can get stomach cancer. I had H-Pylori. Should I also worry about myself? Do I have time? Do I have the energy to worry about my own health?

When I am ninety and my children seventy, will I still worry? Probably. A book I read recently says that worry often reflects a deeper problem, depression. But I am not depressed. I am just worried. Even though I do not believe the book, I worry that I am a worrier. After all, the authorities should know.

28

Reflections on Worry

I think I started to worry when I was just a toddler. I was only five when my mother disappeared for about five days. Looking back now, I think she tried to give my father a lesson about something or other. She believed that absence makes the heart grow fonder. Actually, absence, at least her kind of absence, makes the heart grow angrier. I can still see the image of my father opening the door in our apartment in New York and my mother standing there in her winter coat, this cold silence between them. I always worried about my parents arguing and whether I could make it right somehow.

When I was thirteen years old, my younger brother was born. When he was about two months old, my father protested to my mother that they never went out. So they decided to go out one evening. She took her breast pump along, she always had lots of milk, and left me to baby-sit. About two hours later, my brother woke up, I gave him a bottle and he tried to go back to sleep. As I watched him falling asleep, his eyeballs seemed to roll back into his head. I was frantic. Was he going blind? I kept waking him up to make sure his eyeballs were still in the right place. How could I have known that is the way babies fell asleep?

I have always been a person with strange premonitions that something was wrong. Sometimes I would be haunted for days and I would try, usually unsuccessfully, to bury the worry. But once I had this premonition that something was wrong, that my brother killed himself and this time I was right, he had. He bought a long vacuum hose at Sears, attached it to the car in a friend's garage, turned on the motor and let it run until he died. Now I live on and on with premonitions, never knowing whether they are right or wrong, but haunted by the one time they were right.

We used to have terrible snowstorms in Great Neck, the town I lived in on Long Island. During one of these terrible storms, my younger daughter, Beth, then in high school, went to visit a friend. I remember my near hysteria that she would walk home and an icicle would pierce her body in some way. Even taxis were not working that night. I went, the only car on the road, picked her up and drove slowly home. In an instant, I can recapture all the worry I experienced during that storm.

Probably the most intense and continuous period of worry was my life preceding and right after the divorce. Time helped. At the darkest moments, I would be reassured by telling myself that this problem will be better next year. By this time next year, all these problems will be resolved.

Now many years later, I want to be finally free from worry and these premonitions. What have I to worry about at this stage of life. Death? Illness? Pain? Minor worries, I think, compared to all the other worries I have had in my life. But I can't give up my last worry. Is this writing any good? Is this book funny or crazy? I have no way of knowing and worry that I don't know.

29

Tenants In Common—An Adventure In
Living

The day was one of those sparkling, crisp days in the middle of September. It was 1998, and the sun shone brightly through the glass doors as the early morning dew glistened on the deck and outdoor furniture. The trees were just beginning to turn bright autumn colors and some of the trees dotting the landscape around the house were still green, others were orange and yellow.

Sylvia, a friend for a very long time, and I were in our house, the one we jointly owned in a place called the Springs on the eastern end of Long Island. All our friends were coming later that day to our annual fall party celebrating the return to our house after the summer renters' departure. We shopped the night before and in the early morning were busy preparing for the day, cooking, getting ready for guests, setting the table.

Although we had this "open again" house party every year for almost ten years, I remember this one the most vividly, perhaps because it turned out to be the last one.

The Springs in East Hampton is a small village, north of the main highway on the way to Montauk, on the northeastern end of Long Island. The artists, Jackson Pollack and his wife, Lee Krasner, moved there in 1941. With William DeKooning, they established a setting for the New York School of Painting. Since the release of the film, *Pollack*, many articles about the charm and special characteristics of this small country village have appeared in various newspapers.

Sylvia and I bought our house a half mile away from theirs in 1989. During our purchasing jaunts for a weekend house on the eastern end of Long Island, we fell in love with the Springs, probably for the same reasons they did—the beautiful bays, the unusual light from the sea and the sun, serene quiet, and country-style living. And this section was not as expensive as the rest of the Hamptons.

The image of that day is clear in my mind, Sylvia preparing the main course, chopping the onions, tasting the sauce, moving effortlessly from one task to another. Meanwhile, I set the table, washed the salad ingredients, readied everything else. A gentle spirit of harmony and togetherness flavored everything we did, from cooking to organizing the living room and outside deck for so many people.

Every fall we had this party, and we always had splendid weather, no matter what the weather had been the day before or even that morning. The day would always turn out to be one of those clear sunny days when we could still eat on the deck even in late September or October. The wonderful weather was part of the magic.

Our guests would come for a light lunch, go off to town or the beaches, and come back for cocktails and a potluck supper—sheer Paradise, the myth of the Yellow Kitchen finally realized.

By this time we had grown children and grandchildren. We were both divorced, and the friendship of women was a sustaining force in each of our lives. This house had a special magic and represented a new adventure. We had been friends for many years, worked together on several causes in the town in which we both lived, and we loved this part of Long Island. When we bought the house in 1988 our legal ownership was called "tenants in common," a term used to identify owners of property in equal shares. In case of death, the shares revert to one's heirs instead of to each other.

Both of us lived alone in apartments in Great Neck, Long Island. Both of us sold our homes just before the great real estate boom of the 1980's and neither of us was wise enough to buy an apartment at that time. We craved ownership and a place where we could shape our personal space, furnish, and control it.

Sylvia was executive director of a not-for-profit agency, and I was a college professor, but neither of us could afford to take on the house alone. We were also concerned about loneliness in an area in which we knew no one. It didn't make sense to do it alone financially, or socially.

The plan was to rent the house for the summers to defray costs and use it ourselves for the rest of the year. It was exactly what we wanted. The Springs is more country than beach in topography, and we felt that trees and country would be more fitting for use in the fall, winter, and spring. The house was comfortable for dual ownership because two of the three bedrooms were equal in size.

Friends and family cautioned us about the perils of such an arrangement, but despite all the warnings about joint ownership and future problems, we went ahead with the purchase. And we were right; the problems that people anticipated never came to pass. We did have a formal agreement for deciding disputes, but neither of us looked at it after the original signing.

In two weekends we furnished the entire house, shopping, selecting colors. If she liked this and I preferred something else, we bought both. One weekend we bought all the heavy furniture, beds, bureaus, sofas, chairs. The second weekend we bought all the household items, dishes, pots, towels. We had fun shopping, and it seemed easy to share the costs. We had both been alone for such a long time, we had forgotten how much easier it is for two.

We arranged to have everything arrive on one day. I was there to receive the furniture while she picked up the things that could not be delivered. The first night we had company for dinner. Sylvia's daughter, Janna, was there that night along with my daughter, Beth, and her friend Amy who rode out on their bicycles from New York City and began to put some of the crated furniture together. From the first night we were a family.

There is a special sport in East Hampton, called garage sales. Everyone goes, the rich, the famous, the poor, the elderly, and the newly married. At these garage sales, we bought everything from mirrors, special cooking equipment, a $2 vase, a wonderful chest for $15. We even bought a huge replica of a Robert Duffy painting that needed to be tied to the roof of my car to get it home. That $5 painting dominated our living room all the years we were there.

The walls on three sides of the living-dining room consisted of sliding glass doors. In this house, the outside was part of the living room. We had never before experienced the seasons with such intensity. Our house was bordered by a town preserve, and while we had coffee, read the morning newspaper, or just talked, nature was right outside our windows.

We had to take care of the red carpenter ants or else they would have eaten the foundation, and, eventually, we had to put in a new well. But somehow, these repairs and additions seemed easy to handle, perhaps because we were older and there were two of us now to share the costs, work, and responsibilities.

We loved the wide sandy beaches, the best in the world, the gentle hilly dunes, the panoramic views of the ocean and bays and special topography. The beaches of the Caribbean, southern Italy, or even Cannes do not come close to the fine white sand, the ocean waves against the great expanse of sky, the varied brush, the wild flowers, and the soaring breakers or surf.

I bought a bicycle, my first since adolescence, to roam mostly by myself through the back hills and winding lanes of that part of the peninsula.

On weekends with whatever company came to join us, we took long walks to the bay beaches where one could see as far as Connecticut. On our way to the grandest beach of them all, there was a small cemetery in which Jackson Pollack was buried, a huge rock marked his grave. A little below his was a smaller stone, marking his wife, Lee Krasner, a testimony to gender equity or the lack of it, even in the cemetery.

All my family came to visit from time to time, but it was a yearly ritual, that my son, daughter-in-law, and their family would spend spring vacations with me. They came from Boston, taking the ferry from New London to Orient Point, crossing at Greenport by ferry to Shelter Island, and then by another ferry to Sag harbor. The children loved the idea of three ferries. We would visit all the beaches, set up blankets to ward off the winds, climb the cliffs at Montauk Point, and eat doughnuts at the local bakery.

Sometimes I was out there, sometime Sylvia was there, sometimes we were there together. We each had male companions at that time and we were alone or both couples were there. Friends came and stayed. We cooked together, had the most wonderful meals, and everyone helped with the preparation and cleanup. A cooperative spirit prevailed. It all seemed easy, loving, and satisfying.

Together, we built the foundations of community and intimacy. We built a house of shared values and responsibility. Each weekend had a different flow, a different ambiance depending on who was there. We did not worry about grandchildren, dirt, noise, or messiness. We welcomed those signs of life and new generations.

Our roles evolved. I am good with detail, she was not. I hate to negotiate about money, she was skilled in that area. It was liberating to be able to tell someone that I'm not good at something, without fear of judgment or feelings of inadequacy.

Our lives continued with their peaks, their satisfaction, disappointments—illness, retirement, a child in difficulty—there was always another corner to be turned, another door to open. Some things we could never fix like the lock on the glass doors that drove us crazy. Once, I had to climb in through the bathroom window because the keys didn't work. Each house has its strengths and its vulnerabilities.

"Tenants in common" opened the doors to expanded and creative living. This was not like the house of my youth, nor the house of my life as a married women or single parent. It was not the limited space but physical security of apartment living. This house was modern, light and airy, with nature an essential part of its inner spirit. The sky, birds, and tree-tops were visible through the skylights. Our house was a house of maturity and gratitude for that maturity.

We sold the house in the winter after that last party, having owned it for nine years. I retired and relocated to Boston, Sylvia died the following January. For however long it lasted, it was home, and the symbolism of the yellow kitchen was not a myth, it was real.

30

Adventure and Challenge

I sat there in the middle of boxes, big ones, small ones, and ones too heavy to move. I couldn't find the dining room table anymore and, as I looked around that morning, in 1998, about sixteen years ago, I had this terrible sinking feeling. What was I doing? I was in the throes of two major transitions, retiring from my academic position and relocating to Boston.

I am a born and bred New Yorker and lived there most of my life, except during the early stages of my marriage and when I worked abroad. But the retirement incentive was too good to reject, and my three children, their families, and six grandchildren lived in Boston, a rare coincidence when so many families are dispersed all over the country. The combination retirement and move seemed logical, rational, and timely. That didn't, however, make it easy.

I was doing this alone. Divorce had been the major crisis of my life, but then there were three young children and I had to learn to take care of everything that needed to be done. Now, after so many years in a wonderful career, my academic life was a solid part of my identity, an identity I cherished. Separating from work was difficult, and I had just ended a ten-year relationship.

There was sadness at the thought of leaving life-long friends, friends I'd had since I was young, friends whose children went to nursery school with mine. We were an extended family watching our children grow, marry, and have children of their own. And the communities I belonged to, the Reconstructionist Synagogue of the North Shore and Rabbi Lee Friedlander—his voice and support were a part of my life.

And how would my children feel about me living so close to them? I thought they would be delighted if I was careful about not imposing, but who could be sure of anything?

Even after all I'd been through, after so many years of achievement, independence, and taking risks, moving to a new city was a different story.

But still, the task was to move on.

I was going to create a life of my own, a life of satisfaction, intellectually and socially, a life of independence. While I was tentative about leaving what I had known for so long, I was also intrigued by a new move at this stage of life. Major transitions are both alluring and forbidding.

I was interested in a program at Harvard, the Harvard Institute for Learning in Retirement (HILR). It seemed perfect for me. I could be with peers who shared interests as well as life experiences, and the opportunity to study leisurely and pursue new interests was tantalizing. And since I knew only a few people in Boston, the possibility of making friends through the Harvard program was reassuring.

I had been in the Harvard community before. In the seventies, I was a visiting faculty member for several months at the Harvard Graduate School of Education. In 1990, I had a month-long fellowship through the Association for Religion and Intellectual Life at the Harvard Episcopal Center.

I moved and found a great apartment, joined HILR, and settled in. It soon became clear that I was in a new culture, not the passionate, intense, direct culture of New York, but a setting with a more laid-back, reserved approach. In Boston, I became conscious of holding back, feeling somewhat self-conscious about who I was and my style. But on the whole, the experience was just what I was looking for, and I took advantage of all opportunities. In 2008, four of my peers in the Harvard program and I researched contemporary views of aging and published a book about this stage of life, *New Pathways for Aging*.

Temple Israel in Boston became a spiritual and community home and here too I have branched out and created new spaces for myself and others. I organized a program for older people, and have been involved in many other activities leading to expanding my view of the world and my own life.

Living close to my family after all these years was so different from the several times a year I would travel to Boston or some of my family would travel to New York. Now I could go to soccer games, grandparents' day at school and have dinner with one or all. Over the years, I made friends whom I see on one social level or another. My children are pleased that I have established a life here.

As I look back, there have been life satisfactions and success—at work, in my love life, with friends and family. But there have also been disappointments. I never remarried, although I would have if the right person had come along. There were disappointments at work too. In the last analysis, though, I am resilient whatever the issues, I always take the next step, like the move to Boston.

At the same time, I am constantly reminded of my own mortality—sickness and death are around the corner. It is sobering, baffling, and difficult. Illness and death are also reinforcements that life matters, that each day is important and one must make the most of the moment, physically, intellectually, and emotionally.

These last years have been productive, interesting, and fun. I do feel, though, that I shall always be somewhat of a stranger in Boston. My New York accent betrays me, and none of my history is here. My history is someplace back there in New York, in the houses and apartments of my youth, my marriage, my single-parent period, my life with past lovers, and my career. And, as I said before, "I am still a Yankee fan." But Boston is where I live now, and it is almost home. And living close to family is icing on the cake.

31

On the Sebug River in Connecticut

On her knees
she navigates alone
huddled in her
winter sweater
a buffer against
the early spring wind.

The long, grey, metal canoe
she propels like her body
right, left,
forward now,
keep control.

Rocks gleam on the surface
the river swerves
her heart beats quickly
as she navigates the river
swelled high with melting snows
of early spring
wonder why she's here
challenging the current.

Beguiling white arrows
concealing winter wastes.
pitching in the strong current
spinning in a whirlpool
then smooth like silk.
it suddenly seems so easy.

Around the curve
another torrent to be mastered
a rock, crevice,
fallen branch.
her arms are aching, heavy,
paddle deep, forward now.

She takes control
exulting in the challenge of
the current
then veering toward the
peaceful eddy.

32

Epilogue

The gift of returning to the past led to greater understanding of the present, the one life I have, and my place in a larger scenario.

This book was written over a long period of time. For me, time was needed to face the issues and emotions of those early years with an honesty that only distance can bring. Through my writing I learned to rethink my views of gender, relationships, and identity.

Before the divorce, I tried so hard to be the ideal wife and mother—making drapes, taking cooking lessons, caring for my children, and fulfilling all the fantasies I had of the yellow kitchen. I never thought about what I needed to realize my own abilities.

"Give your husband your pay check," friends advised me when I first started teaching. At that time, my husband, Charly, held a psychology internship in various New York State institutions and did not make much money. But did he really need my paycheck to safeguard his masculinity? And what about my feelings of confidence as a professional and decision-maker? In the fixities and sixties I never disputed the idea of fixed gender roles.

The divorce, such a tragedy for me at that time, became the impetus for growth, independence and the development of my abilities. I did grow, I did change. I moved from the traditional view of a woman's role in the forties and fifties to an independent, professional woman in the seventies, eighties and nineties.

I have been fortunate to have had several long relationships with men after the divorce. With each relationship, I was reminded how men were often socialized to a view of masculinity that was almost impossible to attain. The myths about male sexuality were particularly difficult for them. For me, on the other hand, the feminist movement portrayed models and images that helped me formulate new conceptions of both male and female roles.

This all became clearer to me as I began to write.

I started writing more than thirty years ago when I sold my house and went from room to room remembering what happened there, who we were, and how we developed. Still, it took years before I could embrace writing, years of working hard to keep it all afloat and taking care of the children. Then, there was little time and energy to write. Now, writing fuels my passion and creativity. Often I am at the computer at five in the morning. The gift of returning to the past leads to greater understanding of the present, the one life I have, and my place in a larger scenario.

As I look back over my life, even now many years later, I am reminded again and again of that night long ago when Beth was sick, really sick in the middle of the night and I had to rethink who I was and what I needed to do. Then I found my strength in helping Beth. From where does the strength come now to face the ambiguities ahead?

Sometimes the blessings can get lost in the murkiness of longevity, the shadows of unexpected ailments, the vagueness of where am I going, if anywhere. But each day I try and reconnect with the strength that emerged after the divorce, the force to get a doctorate when I had no money and three young children, and the power to enjoy the magic and mystery of life.

All Grown Up

Beth, Jake and John

Todd, Marian, George and Justin

Stephen and Anne

Michael, Megan, Jonathan

Acknowledgements

My late sister, Milly Kapilow, listened to the recording about "my house," which I made the day before the closing. "This is poetry," she said and transcribed it for me. *The House* was my first writing that was not academic. I have been writing ever since.

Milly kept pushing me to do more, "I will edit, just keep writing," she urged. She died in November, 2008 and I miss her editing, enthusiasm, encouragement and love.

The late Felix Morrow, a publisher, came to my apartment once a week for breakfast; he liked the way I cooked eggs. In return, he would listen to my newest writing, make suggestions and encourage me to keep going. "You have an original voice," he always said, munching away.

Many people have encouraged me since that time. At HILR, Susan Pemsler leads study groups on memoir writing and I have taken three. Her feedback and positive voice always renewed my energy.

A special thank you to Bruce Knobe, also from HILR, who took the photograph of me on the back cover.

Lois Atwood, a genius copy editor and proof reader, is my daughter, Beth's mother-in-law. I am honored that she contributed her talent and skills to my work.

Much gratitude and appreciation to Jennifer Powell, Editor, from

The Excellent Writers Group. She believed in the book from the beginning and always encouraged me to keep going. She has an amazing ability to know what should be expanded and how, and also what might be deleted. "This is worth publishing," she repeated at our biweekly meetings.

Tom Martin has much experience in the publishing world and offered many ideas. A student of mine a long time ago, our roles were now reversed and I followed through on all his suggestions.

Ronald Gross's enthusiasm for this work came at an important moment for me to find the impetus to keep going.

To all the friends, relatives, and special colleagues, too numerous to mention here, who enriched my life in so many ways, a special word of thanks and gratitude.

And finally, to my family who has backed me up in anything and everything.

Rhoada Wald, Summer, 2014

Favorite Memories By My Family

The Atwood Family

John

I remember how Rhoada came rain or shine, sleet or snow to the hospital to let me know how much she loved me.

No one is like Rhoada when it comes to having a party at her house. She can make it interesting, stimulating and lovely. The ultimate introducer.

Watching Rhoada get her new set of knees.

When Beth and I got married we chose a huppa instead of an altar—for Rhoada.

Beth

Mom introduced me to Broadway and ballet – I especially loved seeing *Annie Get Your Gun* for my birthday as well as the New York City Ballet.

I loved the comfort of sleeping in her bed when I was sick—all the way through high school.

Our tradition of making barbecue sauce and hosting an annual barbeque sparerib dinner with garlic bread and lemonade will always be one of my fondest memories.

Mom is terrified of cats and didn't want to go into the basement because a cat had gotten down there.

Mom always made sure to bring us back plenty (20 boxes) of Freihofer cookies when she went to New Paltz.

Going to Jones Beach was one of my favorite activities with my Mom.

Having trouble keeping up with Mom in the pool last year.

Mom can almost out exercise me and her energy is inspiring.

Mom is adventurous and introduced me to white water rafting up in Canada.

Jake

Grandma always makes the best food at her parties especially the desserts.

Grandma always knows the perfect present for me.

I remember when I was little, Grandma would take me to places like the Museum of Science and always explained things to me.

I like when Grandma takes me for Sushi because she knows how much I like it.

The Wald Family

Stephen

Rhoada's Dining Room Table

My mother, Rhoada, had the same dining room table for as long as I can remember. I think it was my grandmother's. It had two pedestals and each descended into three legs. At one time there may have been matching chairs, but not that I recall. There may also have been a sideboard, but I don't recall that either.

Rhoada's table could sit as few as six and it seemed, as many as twenty-five. It came with pads and extra boards that came out for more occasions than anyone can remember. Veneer lifted or disappeared in a half-dozen places.

The table seemed to have an unlimited capacity to hold stuff. Papers and books would sometimes cover the table and stay there for months, or years, but some event eventually intervened to require that the table be cleaned, the extra boards inserted, and the pads brought out.

The kids did their homework, typed school papers, and did projects on the table—although generally a lot fewer than were assigned by their schools.

For what seemed like years, Rhoada's table housed "The Dissertation." In the years before computers, writing a dissertation was, at least from a kid's perspective, about organizing zillions of different kinds of paper, 3×5 cards, 4×8 cards, onion skins, yellow pads, and graph, carbon and typing paper. In the years before electronic copies, backups, and cheap copiers, there was for "The Dissertation" an ever-present threat that something would happen to the papers. The only typed working draft sat in a box on the table always vulnerable to spilled liquids, wild kids when they were young, and intoxicated kids as they got older.

The table was also the place where Rhoada assembled the motliest groups of folks in town. At one time or another, around Rhoada's table, sat an ex-nun married to an ex-priest, ex-rabbi, and ex-communist who spent eighteen months in a federal penitentiary when Roosevelt made a deal to get communist Jews out of the Teamsters, Great Neck folk of every ilk, academics smart as hell, idiots, (many of whom were academics), JAPs (the Jewish, not the Japanese kind), the beach people (Beverly, Sam, etc.) the Woodstock generation, and of course, her tremendously talented and good looking children.

When Rhoada moved to an apartment, the table went to Danvers. Eventually Rhoada followed it there. Grandchildren, the latest generation of tremendously talented and good looking children for whom Rhoada can take credit, now gather around their grandmother at the table, which because of Rhoada everyone assumes will live on after all of us.

Rhoada's Car

The most amazing thing about Rhoada is that she has survived her cars.

Shortly after her divorce, there was this little tin thing that everyone called putt-putt, not because it putt-putted but because it seemed always on the verge of stopping. In the 1960's, almost everyone could identify every car by manufacturer, make, and model year. Somehow, though, I don't remember who made the putt-putt, not even the manufacturer. Everyone remembers, though, that putt-putt had a heater that barely heated, three forward gears, which for those who do not know is a lot less than four or five, a clutch that barely worked, and brakes that were an adventure.

Then came another car of unknown manufacture. There were rumors that it was the last car manufactured in America with a manual transmission with a shifter on the steering column. Then there was a Biscayne, which was the low end in Chevrolet's middle class line. It did everything okay, kind of.

After that came a long line of modestly priced cars that usually did everything they were supposed to, although generally badly.

All the cars had one thing in common, the capacity to be driven thousands and thousands of miles a year for what seemed like forever. Rhoada drove countless miles, every day for a couple of years to Columbia, a trip New Yorkers know takes somewhere between forty minutes and three hours, then from Great Neck to New Paltz, then to Saratoga, then to Boston, sometimes in snow, often early in the morning, real early, and often at night.

Her grandchildren know she now drives a Toyota. They have no idea.

Anne

I remember when shortly after graduation from Vassar, after way too much recreational fortification, I finally got up the courage to call Essex Road at two in the morning to tell Stephen Wald that I didn't like the fact that he was ignoring me. Rhoada, half groggy with sleep, answered the phone and said, actually a bit cautiously, but not grudgingly, "Sure, I'll get him."

Something inside me said, "Yes, now I know, why he is the way he is. And, I like it."

I remember that Rhoada upon every memorable event in her children's lives, graduations from graduate schools, weddings, births, always appeared so radiant with joy and happiness and life, that I would just gaze at her and know that I too would feel that joy with my own children some day...if her son ever got up the courage to ask me to marry him.

I remember watching her pack for India and how nervous and excited she was. She was traveling to a new continent, alone, and her normal anxiety never overcame her extraordinary courage. She wrote us interesting and loving missives that I still have and still treasure.

I remember every trip to Schenck Ave. I loved visiting Rhoada there. I loved walking up the pathways on cold November nights after driving five hours with three small children and seeing the lights from her kitchen window. I loved the idea that her apartment was so warm that we had to keep the windows open to keep ourselves from overheating. I loved the fact that sleeping quarters were always available for any combination of adults and children. I loved the fact that her kitchen was so tiny and fed scores. I loved the fact that she always remembered your favorite foods...like the bagel twists, dozens of them, the bagels, the juice boxes, the fried chicken...the half moon cookies, the mondel bread, all because you were coming and she wanted to make you happy.

I loved the fact that she always invited her friends to see us...to come over...to be another guest at the celebration. I would gaze at her again and once more see the joy, love, and happiness as she swept up the cheerios and told us to "never mind" about the apple juice or urine on the pull-out sofa.

Megan

I loved that you were able to visit me in St. Louis and will always remember sitting outside with you and my Mom, eating tapas and drinking sangria at Barcelona.

Who could ever forget climbing that mountain on the elder hostel trip? Or perhaps the play you seemed to just pull together for the group to act out?

Many memories from Great Neck...

- Running and jumping on the awesome merry-go-round at the park down the street, even though you and my Mom would yell at me.

- Trying my very first everything bagel (I have yet to find anything as delicious as those).

- You letting me chop onions in your tiny kitchen because I thought I was strong enough to cut them without crying. I don't think it was successful, but oh well, thank God my "I can do anything" phase has passed.

Pink boots—really not much more to say except that they are still wonderful.

Eating dinner in Somerville with you and Todd. I hope we can make sure it happens again—nothing is better than that.

And lastly, I will never forget analyzing the concept of "hooking up" during the course of our most recent adventure from NY to Boston.

Jonathan

I remember....

Going out to lunch with Grandma at Walden Pond.

When we went to Blue Man Group.

Going to the beaches on Long Island and playing in the gravel driveway.

Looking for the matzoh every year at Grandma's house and always losing to Jake.

Going to Jones Beach.

When Grandma moved into her new apartment.

Michael

When Grandma took Jon and me to the Blue Man Group in Boston. All three of us got really scared when one of the guys started getting closer and closer to us every time the lights went out. He ended up getting so close that after the show Grandma told me that I had some blue paint on my face.

Going to the beach with Grandma in East Hampton.

I remember taking the tour of Grandma's new apartment in Brookline for the first time and thinking about how much more I liked her apartment in New York because I was familiar with it. Yet,

I was also thinking that wasn't important because Grandma would now be only a fifteen minute trip from our house.

I remember how happy Grandma was when we surprised her with a new computer.

The Myers Family

George

When I think of Rhoada I think of

Her strong spirit—bicycles, kayaks, swimming

Times in New Hampshire, Thanksgiving, Danvers, and Passover dinners

Connections—Willing to leave New York for Boston to be with her family.

I think of brisket, Harvard, and "everything on them bagels" from N.Y.

Marian

Sleeping by the fireplace on Essex Rd. when the lights went out.

We drove around in a car that could not go up hills. We called it "miniature putt putt." Even though it was the only car we could afford, you made it fun.

All the fun we had at my wedding when we stayed at the Sonesta Hotel and you jogged six miles to my house in Brookline.

We went camping and I locked the keys in the trunk of the car. You managed to get someone to help us.

We drove to Florida with Aunt Milly and Grandma. I loved the drive especially the funny Mexican place that had signs for 200 miles. I also remember the red ants.

Being afraid to go into the basement because the boiler might blow up.

Always having someone new at our holiday dinners. It was usually someone who had no place to go or was experiencing the first Passover Seder. People always felt welcome and wanted in our home.

Todd

Playing hearts with Grandma on our camping trip.

Grandma figured out the complicated remote control in New Hampshire after everyone else had long given up.

Having Grandma's incredibly good brisket so many times.

Getting severe static shock in Grandma's New York apartment.

I remember her apartment being covered with pictures from India.

I remember Grandma's apartment building in New York having an amazing echo and yelling to hear the echo and then bothering her neighbors.

Justin

One of my favorite memories of Grandma was when I took her down the bike trail near our house in New Hampshire. What made it so special to me was the responsibility I felt she had given me that day.

Besides being cozy places to stay, your apartments, both past and present, have been decorated with memorabilia that has educated me about Middle Eastern Jewish life.

Your home has been very much like a family museum to me and makes me feel like I have my own background and culture.

I will never forget the day I stood on top of the ten foot diving board at your swimming pool. To this day I regret not jumping.

Remember the Sunday we had your friend Muriel from Israel over for dinner. For me, once again the exposure to another culture and way of life made this memory special. Remember when she yelled at me for asking too many questions?

Author Profile

What happens when the dream of "living happily ever after" turns into a nightmare? At thirty-seven, Rhoada Wald thought her life was unfolding exactly as it should until her husband unexpectedly demanded a divorce and left her to raise three young children on her own. Faced with the sudden disruption of her youthful dreams, she took charge and reshaped her life.

The Myth of the Yellow Kitchen begins with the devastation of divorce and moves to the transformation of a young wife and mother into a mature professional woman. How did she get from there to here? Her memoir is a compelling testimony that follows the ups and downs of her passage from life-changing crisis to a pioneering career in non-traditional higher education and new experiences and adventures.

Dr. Wald's doctoral degree is from Teachers College, Columbia University. She specialized in innovative education for adults at Empire State College, a unit of the State University of New York. Since its inception in 1972, the College has been on the cutting edge of new directions in non-traditional higher education and Dr. Wald played a pivotal role in that development both in this country and abroad.

A winner of the Chancellor's Award for Excellence in Teaching (SUNY) as well as a recipient of a Fulbright Travel Award, she taught for extended periods in India, Cyprus and Israel.

The Myth of the Yellow Kitchen represents a turning point in her life and her writing. She moved from academic writing to a highly readable, eloquent journey about life and work. In a non-bitter, affirming, and often humorous voice, the book evokes optimism and affirmation.

Dr. Wald relocated to Boston from New York in 1999 where her three children and their families live. In Boston, she has been active in several institutions of higher education, specializing in learning during retirement. She is one of the authors of *New Pathways for Aging* published in 2008 by the Harvard Institute for Learning in Retirement (HILR).

CPSIA information can be obtained at www.ICGtesting.com
Printed in the USA
BVOW03s1608150914

366582BV00001B/2/P